You'll Never Walk Alone

A Daily Guide to Renewal

You'll Never Walk Alone

A Daily Guide to Renewal

Ronald E. Minor

PARACLETE PRESS
BREWSTER, MASSACHUSETTS

Library of Congress Cataloging–in–Publication Data
Minor, Ronald E., 1936–
    You'll never walk alone : a daily guide to renewal / Ronald E. Minor
        p. cm.
    ISBN 1–55725–360–9 (pbk.)
    1. Spiritual life—Christianity. I. Title.
    BV4501.3.M57 2004
    248.4—dc22
                                                        2003022817

10 9 8 7 6 5 4 3 2 1

© 2004 by Ronald E. Minor

ISBN 1-55725-360-9

Published by Paraclete Press
Brewster, Massachusetts
www.paracletepress.com

Printed in the United States of America.

CONTENTS

INTRODUCTION

This book is intended to be a guide for the next twelve weeks of your journey—an encouragement to you who are feeling alone, distressed, or challenged beyond your comfort zone. Some years ago I stood along the route of the Boston Marathon, watching brave and weary runners slogging up "Heartbreak Hill." We knew that once they reached the top of this hill the route was basically downhill and usually downwind to the finish line. Stationed along that challenging incline was a cadre of supportive people, calling out encouragement to each faltering runner—holding out cups of cold water or orange sections to be grasped on the run. I hope that this book will be just that for you—an encouragement to the weary, "a rest upon the way," a prod for those who long nostalgically for a life without struggle, a call to keep going, an assurance that you can make it regardless of how you feel at the moment.

I hope that these devotional helps will give expression to some of your unspoken feelings and call you on in the confidence that you can explore new dimensions of faith and love. These are written so that you can take this part of your journey by yourself if you choose to. They are also arranged to be helpful for those who can answer the questions, found at the end of each days reading, in a supportive group setting—perhaps even in a group intentionally formed to consider these together.

Walking day by day with God offers us ever-new challenges in myriad circumstantial settings. God promises to constantly renew our faith as we onward go. My prayer is that these devotions and questions will be a resource for renewing your faith in the weeks ahead and for enhancing the value of your journey with God.

Our Confidence is in the Lord

A VERSE FOR THE WEEK
"Fear not, for I have redeemed you;
I have called you by name; you are mine."
(Isaiah 43:1b)

Why am I Afraid?

DAILY READING   Proverbs 3:1–18

VERSES TO FOCUS OUR THOUGHTS
Trust in the LORD with all your heart
and lean not on your own understanding;
in all your ways acknowledge him,
and he will make your paths straight.
(vv. 5-6)

In these verses God gives us a sense of security. He will make our own crooked paths into his straight paths. He will go before us and prepare our way. He is with us on the trail. The condition upon which all this will happen is our trusting in the Lord—with all our hearts. How often we are fearful and anxious! Is this because we don't really trust God's love? Is it because we try to figure everything out for ourselves? As great, or as weak, as we still look to ourselves—as secure or as uncertain as we may yet feel, we naturally want to trust ourselves, and to that extent our life is based on a lie—the lie that we can take care of ourselves, we can find our own way.

I discovered that the reason I didn't trust God is that I didn't really believe that he loves me in the depth of my being. In other words, the level of my anxiety ran deeper than my love for God. I had sung, "Jesus loves me, this I know, for the Bible tells me so," since I was a child, yet on the deeper level of my anxieties I didn't know that it was true.

John tells us, "There is no fear in love. But perfect love drives out fear"(1 John 4:18a). Love is not just greater than fear, it actively drives away fear—gets rid of it. God desires that we hear him constantly telling us that he loves us—that he has redeemed us—that he calls us by name, telling us again and again that we belong to him. We are safe. His love is greater than all our fears.

3

For one whole year I woke up each morning to hear God telling me specifically that he loved me. At first I was suspicious that I was just making this up because I so desperately wanted to hear it. Finally I came to know deep in my spirit that his love *was* greater than my growing anxieties, and I received a lasting peace. What a relief to know that my anxieties no longer needed to rule my life.

> *1. Do you still believe that you ought to be able to take care of yourself—to run your own life? Only God can truly take care of you. Ask him to show you that you are safe in his care.*
> *2. God wants us to know that he loves us. Listen for him to tell you that he loves you and believe it with all your heart.*

DAY TWO
What Are Our Real Fears?

DAILY READING   Psalm 103:1–18

VERSES TO FOCUS OUR THOUGHTS
Praise the LORD . . .
He forgives all my sins and heals all my diseases. . . .
(vv. 1, 3)

We all have our fears. Some of us are more aware of this than others, and some are more fearful than others, but all of us need help in trusting. Fears can be as specific as the fear of snakes, or the fear of going blind, or the fear of the "boogie man." These fears often come from scarring experiences in our early childhood, or scary stories we have heard, or movies we have seen at impressionable moments in our development.

Fears can be as general as the fear of darkness or loud noises or certain types of people. Again this may stem from difficult childhood experiences or from post-traumatic syndromes originating in later life. Fears can further develop into unfocused anxieties that engulf us without detectable warning signs. Waking up in the middle of the night, we discover a pervading feeling of dread. Even when we are doing something as pleasurable as walking in the woods on a beautiful afternoon, we can become suddenly gripped by undefined panic.

Fear is a lack of faith, the inability or unwillingness to trust God in an area of our lives. Fear can act like a disease within us—like a cancer quietly taking over inside and crippling us. Like a cancer it originates from a specific source. Therefore, it is important to discover our fears—to locate them specifically, to name them, to find out where they originated and what caused them.

God tells us that he will "forgive all our sins and heal all our diseases." So when we can identify our fears and talk about them until we can fully own them, we can then offer them to God for his forgiveness and healing. He desires to deliver us completely from all childhood and adulthood traumas.

1. Do you know what your specific fears are? Ask God to reveal them to you if you are unable to name them.
2. Can you talk about these with a close friend? Often if we talk about them, they lose their power over us because we discover where they came from, and we can specifically give them over to God for his healing.

DAY THREE
What Feeds Our Fears?

DAILY READING   Matthew 6:25–34

A VERSE TO FOCUS OUR THOUGHTS
But seek first his kingdom and his righteousness,
and all these things will be given to you as well.
(v. 33)

O nce we admit that we are fearful and can begin to identify
some of our fears, we may then discover that we feel
comfortable with them and would actually prefer to keep them.
We may feel that they have served us well. We may even feed
them.

Fears serve our selfish wants and demands. They can become
ways of attempting to control the unknown, to anticipate the
scary future, to prepare ourselves fatalistically for bad things to
happen to us, to keep ourselves from being blindsided by a force
larger than ourselves, namely God.

These are all symptoms that we still prefer our more
"comfortable" ways, our pleasures, our will to God's will for our
lives. Fears become a method of protecting ourselves from
following God, whom we find difficult to trust. Even as
Christians we camouflage this excuse for not seeking his
kingdom first—by accusing him of not caring. We withdraw
into our self-justifying fears, and we slander God's character by
acting as if he didn't love us. When we can see our fears from this
self-serving perspective, is it any wonder that we have remained
anxious?

In the Sermon on the Mount, Jesus speaks to people who
are accustomed to living according to their fears. "Who of you
by worrying can add a single hour to his life?" Jesus asks
(Matthew 6:27). He calls us to look at the birds in the air or the
flowers in the fields, and to see how his Father cares for them.
How much more does he care for us! He calls us to trust him

and to seek his kingdom, and all our needs will be met. Putting his will ahead of our own, we will lose our fears of the future or of anything else.

1. Does it feel safer to fear than to trust? Have you used your fears in an attempt to get something under control?
2. Ask God to forgive you for your specific fears and to give you a new gift of faith.

DAY FOUR
What Am I Afraid to Lose?

DAILY READING   Philippians 3:7–14

A VERSE TO FOCUS OUR THOUGHTS
I consider everything a loss compared to the
surpassing greatness of knowing Christ Jesus my Lord,
for whose sake I have lost all things.
(v. 8b)

What are you most afraid to lose? For most of us, losing control of our lives is the most threatening thing we can imagine. We don't want other people telling us what to do for fear that they will take us over. This is especially true if you are like me and had a domineering parent for whom you compromised your individuality and gave over unwarranted control.

In a real sense we are not to give over control of our lives to another person, unless God has directed us to do so for a specific season for specific help. But we are definitely commanded to give over control of our lives to God. And here is the rub.

He is our creator. We belong to him both by creation and by redemption. We are his, and he has the right to direct every area of our lives. Wherever we are "holding out" on God, whatever we consider "off-limits" for him, is where our anxiety is rooted. Do we have a questionable relationship that we have told him is none of his business? Do we have an offensive addiction that we refuse to give up? Do we demand a certain career path or educational plan that he had better not challenge?

Years ago Robert Boyd Munger wrote a little allegory called "My Heart Christ's Home," in which he compares our heart to a home. When we invite Jesus to live in our heart, he becomes our guest and will be content for a time to occupy that part of our heart that we offer to him. But he patiently and persistently waits for all of it. In Munger's story the occupancy question finally focused on one locked closet that was beginning to smell, and which the owner refused to unlock. The closet represents the last place we are holding out on God in our lives. It represents our independence—having some control over our lives. Soon the person in the allegory discovered that the independence that he was most afraid to lose was where his fear was rooted. Once yielded, the fear generated by self-protection was gone. Only when the whole heart was given over and made available to Jesus, was there peace.

1. Is there an area of your life that you have locked against the presence and will of Jesus—a place that you feel should be none of his business?
2. What steps do you need to take in order to give this place over to him? This may take time, so ask him to assist you step by step.

DAY FIVE

What Am I Afraid to Gain?

DAILY READING Philippians 1:18b–26

A VERSE TO FOCUS OUR THOUGHTS
For to me, to live is Christ
and to die is gain.
(v. 21)

What are we afraid to gain? This is the more difficult question to answer. Most of us can more readily identify fear with loss than we can with gain. So this may be an even more revealing question for us to consider. We tend to sacrifice freedom for security, to sacrifice expansion for safety.

God may desire to bless us through what looks like a risky relationship. He may want to liberate us through a new level of honesty with key people in our lives. He may wish to increase our level of responsibility through a job promotion, or by calling us to take a more public profile. Are we willing to respond to his call to these kinds of "gains"? We often spend much energy, and we experience much fear, choosing to live our lives in a safer and better known arena, when God is calling us on to new things.

In yesterday's passage from Philippians, Paul declared that he was willing to lose—actually had lost—all things in order to gain Christ. In today's passage, again from Philippians, he declares that he will trust God with every "gain." Paul trusted God so thoroughly—he had found him so faithful in every new adventure, every hardship—that he could confidently say, "Do not be anxious about anything" that God asks you to do (Philippians. 4:6). You can follow him safely anywhere that he calls you. You can step out of every safe boat from which he summons you. Even the "gain" of death held no fear for Paul, and it need hold no fear for us. Every call of God is a gain.

1. Do you hide away in the shadows for fear of being asked to do something that you aren't sure you can do? Has God asked anything of you that you are not willing to step forward and "gain"?

2. Ask God to show you that holding back produces more anxiety than stepping forward into his new life.

DAY SIX

Making Friends with Our Fears

DAILY READING Psalm 111:1–10

A VERSE TO FOCUS OUR THOUGHTS
The fear of the Lord is the beginning of wisdom.
(v. 10a)

After all our consideration of the negative aspects of fear and how it saps our spiritual energy, it may seem paradoxical to now think of fear as actually being a "friend." Perhaps it would be helpful in this instance to think of fear or anxiety as being like spiritual pain.

Physical pain is uncomfortable, and we may unwisely wish that we didn't have to endure it. However, those who, through nerve damage or other physical deficiencies, have lost the ability to feel pain know the great protective value of this warning system. People find themselves in grave danger because they can't tell when they are in trouble until it may be too late for a simple remedy.

In a similar way fear, as spiritual pain, alerts us that there is something wrong spiritually, and the discomfort we feel is intended to prompt us to take action. Since we all experience fear and anxiety to some degree, this should not make us feel that we are inferior Christians, but it does point to an area of our life that needs our attention. It is a warning light on the dashboard of faith. In this way God uses even our fear to our advantage, and wisdom begins when we consider fear to be God's prompting us to change.

Now let us look at fear as a friend in a different light. The psalmist writes, "The fear of the Lord is the beginning of wisdom" (Psalm 111:10a). This, and other passages like it, refers to fear as a healthy respect, an attitude of reverence, a sense of awe in the presence of almighty God. God wants us to take him seriously. He cannot be compromised—he cannot be trivialized or discounted or avoided or devalued. God is God. Wisdom begins when we learn to fear God in this way. We should consider this kind of fear also as a friend because it leads us into the truth of our relationship with God and enables us to take him seriously.

1. If you are experiencing fear or anxiety, ask God to show you what he wants to change in your life.

2. Ask him to give you a true appreciation of who he is—a loving heavenly Father who plans only good for his children.

DAY SEVEN
Fearlessness and How to Get There

DAILY READING   Psalm 27:1–14

A VERSE TO FOCUS OUR THOUGHTS
The Lord is my light and my salvation–whom shall I fear?
The Lord is the stronghold of my life—of whom shall I be afraid?
(v. 1)

Let the person who is without fear please stand up. Fear is something that we all experience, especially during our childhood. During our teenage years and into early adulthood we may invent methods for camouflaging these feelings, and we may even perform daring feats in an attempt to prove our fearlessness to ourselves and to others. But underneath our cool facade, anxiety is still present. As we grow older, and our compensating energies wane, and medical and other life-threatening realities emerge, our fears no longer remain compliant. I am discovering as I approach my more mature years that heretofore hidden fears are surfacing. It is time to face these and give them over to God.

Fearlessness is not a technique for brave people. Fearlessness is the result of facing our fears, working through them, and coming to peace with God. Fearlessness is based on experiential confidence in Jesus and what he was and is willing to do for us. Fearlessness comes from laying down every area, every relationship, every secret ambition, every dear possession before him and saying, "Your will be done." Fearlessness comes when we entrust our whole lives into his loving hands.

When we have nothing left to protect, when we truly are in awe of God, then there is no need to fear people or situations. When we clearly hear God speaking and know his will for us, other challenges can no longer threaten us. When we know how much he loves us, when the Lord is the stronghold of our lives, of whom shall we be afraid?

This was the testimony that Jesus had. He knew how much his heavenly Father loved him. He was totally committed to doing his Father's will. So he went forward to the cross with grief and much pain, but without fear. Once he had wrestled with his Father in the Garden of Gethsemane and knew for sure that this was his Father's will for him, he was at peace in the midst of the greatest challenges and opposition.

1. Is it possible for the Lord to be the "stronghold" in your present situation—to see him as bigger, more powerful, more caring than any situation or other person of whom you are afraid?

2. Is there an area of your life in which you need to wrestle something out with God until you know his will and can trust in his love?

God is by Our Side

"[Jesus said] You will leave me all alone.
Yet I am not alone, for my Father is with me."
(John 16:32b)

Traumatized, Rejected, and Abandoned

DAILY READING   Hebrews 13:1–16

A VERSE TO FOCUS OUR THOUGHTS
God has said, "Never will I leave you;
never will I forsake you."
(v. 5b)

I wonder why I feel so lonely at times when there are lots of people around, and I have a good family and good friends. But is there really someone there for me—someone who notices, who cares, who is not too busy? Recently when I was wrestling through another bout of depression all those feelings came rushing up again.

I'm sure that I am not the only one who struggles with an irrational sense of loneliness. Our society is becoming more and more isolating. Supportive neighborhoods and caring extended families are disappearing. Members of smaller nuclear families live separated lives. Even the common evening meal is a rare occurrence. Television has taken the place of relationships with real people. Some married couples prefer to watch TV alone, in separate parts of the house. How do we handle our increased feelings of isolation? Let us first look at some deeper causes for this feeling of aloneness.

Feelings of rejection and abandonment are often the result of things that have been done to us in the past. Our private traumas isolate us and cause us to feel lonely. It is common today to have delayed remembrances of sexual, physical, or emotional abuse that occurred to us in childhood. Being given up for adoption, having our parents separate and divorce, an ill-timed family move, or the untimely death of a close friend or relative, are other significant isolating experiences.

Hurtful events, including childhood sicknesses with debilitating consequences, cause us to bury hurts as we attempt to live around the inner sense of loneliness. It is possible that we may never have spoken about these things to anyone. Maybe we were threatened by perpetrators not to speak of them, nevertheless they left us in pain—feeling somehow less acceptable and alone to cope with our damaged lives.

But now as adult Christians we understand that Jesus was there with us, because he has told us that he has never abandoned us, never forsaken us. He has always been with us, and he understands. Jesus experienced severe trauma and felt totally abandoned by his followers as he went to the cross. "You will leave me all alone," he told them. But he knew he was not alone, "for my Father is with me" (John 16:32). That truth is what sustained him.

1. Will you entrust your unhealed traumas into the loving care of a heavenly Father who has promised to heal you?
2. Perhaps you would benefit from talking about your painful experiences and from receiving the healing prayer that could welcome Jesus into those places where you have felt, and continue to feel, so alone.

DAY TWO

Feeling Sorry for Ourselves and Not Forgiving:
Increasing our Loneliness

DAILY READING 2 Timothy 4:9–18

VERSES TO FOCUS OUR THOUGHTS
At my first defense, no one came to my support,
but everyone deserted me. May it not be held against them.
But the Lord stood at my side and gave me strength.
(vv. 16-17)

I had a dear older friend who had been "cheated" out of his inheritance by a questionable legal move on the part of his father's second wife. I spent several evenings sitting at a summer campfire with him, listening to his story and encouraging him to try to forgive her. I hoped that he could understand that forgiving her would not make her right, and that it could free him from the emotional prison of this trauma. As far as I know he never could accept that and remained a lonely man. Remaining the victim and continuing to blame others for our pain may cause us to forfeit a sense of God's love and forgiveness.

If we continue to feel sorry for ourselves, we will not be able to forgive others. Unforgiveness and self-pity seem to travel together. They maximize our hurts and traumas and keep them alive in us long after we might have been healed. In effect, we build protective walls around our hurts so that others can't help us. Rather than releasing ourselves from past hurts we hang onto them, even nurse them, as we see life from a wrong perspective. When we look back over our life's journey with God, according to the familiar imagery of the footprints in the sand, we generally see two sets of prints. When there is only a single set of tracks visible, we are quick

19

to accuse God of abandoning us in our need. To our chagrin God reminds us that those were the precise times when he carried us through our traumas.

In today's verses from Timothy, Paul explains how he felt humanly abandoned at a crucial junction in his life. "Everyone deserted me" (4:16). But there is no sense of a binding self-pity here, because he quickly forgave them. How could he do this? He was so sure that the Lord had not abandoned him—"he stood at my side and gave me strength," that for him human hurts were not worth hanging onto.

1. Have you been deeply hurt by someone? Forgiving her or him would release their hold on you. Perhaps that could be a goal for the remaining weeks of this devotional.
2. Will you believe that God wants to change your perspective and replace your loneliness with a sense of his sustaining presence?

DAY THREE
Alone in a Crowd

DAILY READING   Romans 5:6–11

A VERSE TO FOCUS OUR THOUGHTS
But God demonstrates his own love for us in this:
While we were still sinners, Christ died for us.
(v. 8)

I am acutely aware that superficial relationships can be more painful than no relationship at all, because they awaken unfulfilled expectations. Families and especially marriages are thought to be permanent cures for loneliness, but it is possible that they may in effect only exaggerate our feelings. Being unable to connect emotionally with either of my parents left me longing for relationships even in the midst of a large family.

To this day I have to fight against feeling rejected by people who are not prepared to connect with me emotionally.

There was a woman in the crowd who was not part of the crowd that surrounded Jesus one day. She had been traumatized through years of suffering from a socially unacceptable medical condition. Her intention was to sneak through the crowd, touch Jesus' garment and quickly vanish before she could be detected. But Jesus, in his love for her, called her out of the crowd and publicly announced her healing to everyone. Her embarrassment at being found out was quickly swallowed up by a new sense of acceptability. She was healed emotionally as well as physically.

We think of ourselves as being socially unacceptable for a great variety of reasons. Like this unnamed woman we are afraid of "being found out." We mask ourselves, feeling safer as the "Lone Ranger." In our fear of rejection, we pre-reject ourselves and then project these feelings onto our friends. I have discovered that when I have been honest about my feelings or embarrassing situations in my life, other Christians have been waiting to discover the real me! I have been blessed to find out that people would prefer to know the weak me rather than the more put-together image I project.

How wonderful when we can truly believe that God has already accepted us just the way we are! Paul assures us, "While we were still sinners, Christ died for us" (Romans 5:8b). We did nothing to earn his love, nothing to gain his acceptance. God knows all about us, and still he accepts us unconditionally. That's amazing love. This frees us to trust other Christians to know us as we really are.

1. It is often difficult to believe that God accepts us totally as we are. Are you willing to ask God to reveal himself to you on a deeper level?
2. As you are learning to trust other people, is there another level of honesty about which you can share?

DAY FOUR

The Rhythm of Times Together and Times Alone

DAILY READING Mark 6:31–46

A VERSE TO FOCUS OUR THOUGHTS
Then, because so many people were coming and going
that they did not even have a chance to eat, he said to them,
"Come with me by yourselves to a quiet place and get some rest."
(v. 31)

Have you noticed how Jesus was always surrounded by people? He lived within an amazing swirl of activity and demand, having no place of his own to which he could retire and shut out the world. Aside from the initial forty-day period of temptation and the trip up the Mount of Transfiguration with three of his disciples, we have no record of his taking any long-term retreat. Yet Jesus continually found time for private conversations with his Father. He went alone to pray despite the pressure to teach and to heal the sick. We are told that he would rise "very early in the morning, while it was still dark . . . and [go] off to a solitary place, where he prayed" (Mark 1:35).

On several occasions Jesus encouraged his disciples to follow the same pattern, inviting them to "Come with me by yourselves to a quiet place and get some rest" (Mark 6:31). Isn't it wonderful that this invitation extends to you and to me?

We, too, are encouraged to establish patterns of quiet, even "lonely times." Dedicating a few moments each morning (or later in the day) to being with our heavenly Father, so we can hear him speaking with us before the clamoring of the daily round of busyness begins, is the gift that Jesus offers when he says, "Come with me by yourselves." In this way we can attune our hearts to hear his voice.

1. Even though you have a demanding schedule, are there a few moments during the day that you could find to "Come away and be with [God] by yourself?"
2. Make a realistic goal for how long this daily devotional time will be. For some it will be a few minutes; for some it will be more. Try to keep to your schedule for a week.

DAY FIVE

The Fear of Being Alone with God

DAILY READING   Exodus 19:9b–25

VERSES TO FOCUS OUR THOUGHTS
"When my glory passes by, I will put you in a cleft in the rock
and I cover you with my hand until I have passed by.
Then I will remove my hand and you shall see my back;
but my face must not be seen."
(Exodus 33:22-23)

S ome years ago I went to a retreat house, having dedicated a few days to be together with several close friends. At our initial meeting with the retreat master it was suggested that we each experience a private retreat. This meant spending three days in a private hermitage alone, with our individual meals being brought to us. This was a gracious offer, but my spontaneous reaction was to panic. I had been looking for a time of fellowship, and as much as I like quietness, I didn't want to be totally alone with God—and I was embarrassed to admit this.

We are not naturally comfortable with ourselves or with God. Take away the people and our outside stimuli, leave us alone for an extended period of time, and we may well experience panic. We are, most of us, afraid of being alone with God—all for different reasons. During those three days, I faced some of mine.

Moses experienced the awesomeness of God on Mt. Sinai. God placed him in the cleft of a rock and covered him with his hand so that he would not be overcome by his glory. No wonder we are so fearful! But in Jesus, who has wonderfully opened the way for us to come into his Father's presence, we can come with wonder, but without anxiety. It is in this time of aloneness with God that the Apostle Paul tells us, "We all with unveiled face, beholding the glory of the Lord, are being changed into his likeness from one degree of glory to another" (2 Corinthians 3:18 RSV).

Being alone with God proved to be a rich experience— though scary—for me on that retreat years ago. But I discovered that each step we take toward aloneness before God is worth seeking out.

1. When you think of days alone before God, how do you respond? Perhaps you would like to look at the possible reasons for this.

2. There are other invitations in God's Word in which he encourages us to come to him, to be alone with him. Can you think of at least three of these?

DAY SIX
Seeking God Out

DAILY READING 1 Kings 19:9b–18

VERSES TO FOCUS OUR THOUGHTS
After the earthquake came a fire, but the Lord was not in the fire.
And after the fire came a gentle whisper.
When Elijah heard it, he pulled his cloak over his face and went out and stood at the mouth of the cave.
(vv. 12-13)

From time to time God asks us to spend some additional time alone with him. It feels as if he cuts us out of the pack, so to speak, for a time—a day or a few days—so that he can make his way better known to us. It is important to hear God for ourselves. As the old spiritual reminds us:

We must walk the lonesome valley;
we must walk it by ourselves.
Nobody else can walk it for us;
we must walk it by ourselves.

Moses returned to the presence of God on Mt. Sinai alone, leaving even his assistant Joshua behind at the base of the mountain. Jacob wrestled with the angel at the ford of the Jabbok alone, having sent his whole entourage on ahead. Jesus in the Garden of Gethsemane encouraged three of his disciples to watch with him, but they were not prepared to share his agony.

Elijah met God at Mt. Horeb alone, after he had run away from Jezebel. He had traveled for forty days and forty nights. He was troubled. He spread his complaints—his feelings of loneliness—his sense of failure—before God. After several great natural events, Elijah could hear God speaking in a gentle whisper, and his life took a whole new direction.

Sometimes God calls us to withdraw physically, or at least interiorly, and to hear his voice for ourselves. A crisis in our lives may suggest the timing, unanswered questions may prompt it, a spiritual director might encourage it. We may be afraid that we can't hear anything, or afraid to take responsibility for what we do hear, but these times will be the hinges upon which our lives may swing.

When it comes to major decisions—turning points in our lives—hearing God for ourselves is a privilege we can't afford to miss. Taking another person's word is risky. Besides, God loves to tell us himself.

1. Do you have unanswered questions in your life at the moment? Are you looking for new direction? Perhaps it is time for a new step of faith.

2. Are you willing to believe that he will answer if you ask him, and that you can hear his voice? When you ask him, trust what you hear.

DAY SEVEN
Solitude

DAILY READING John 16:25–33

A VERSE TO FOCUS OUR THOUGHTS
[Jesus said,] "You will leave me all alone.
Yet I am not alone, for my Father is with me."
(v. 32b)

Solitude is the positive form of aloneness or loneliness. It is possible to be alone without being lonely. We can be at peace within ourselves, and therefore at peace in our aloneness. A deeper settledness inside gives us the freedom either to be alone or with other people, with equal ease.

Jesus knew that when people abandoned him, when he was left "all alone," he was no more alone than when they were with him. He knew that his Father was with him and would never leave him. His relationship with his Father sustained him. We too can cultivate this kind of intimate relationship with our heavenly Father.

Webster's College Dictionary defines solitude as seclusion, remoteness from habitation, a lonely or unfrequented place. Most likely we are not called to be hermits, and we may not be able to sustain a silent lifestyle, but we can have a quiet place in our hearts, where we can withdraw and be with Jesus. Orthodox mystics often refer to "withdrawing into our hearts," or to "having our minds descend into our hearts" to be alone there with Jesus. This refers to the deeper communication of the Spirit—fellowship that bypasses our thought processes and relates to God spirit to Spirit. The mystics understand that we can have a hermitage in our hearts where we are in abiding and sustaining fellowship with God.

This deeper communion can be encouraged through spending time in God's presence, listening to his voice, trusting in what we hear. This is the ultimate antidote for our feelings of loneliness, and it is the fulfillment of aloneness.

1. Spending a little time quietly listening to God each day is a helpful practice. Are you willing to give it a try this week?
2. It is further helpful to have a notebook and to write down what you hear each day. It is amazing how much more believable God's words are to you when you see them in writing.

God Accepts Us Just As We Are

A VERSE FOR THE WEEK
But God demonstrates his own love for us in this:
While we were still sinners, Christ died for us.
(Romans 5:8)

Why Do We Find it Difficult to Accept Ourselves?

DAILY READING Matthew 9:9–13

VERSES TO FOCUS OUR THOUGHTS
It is not the healthy who need a doctor, but the sick.
But go and learn what this means:
"I desire mercy, not sacrifice."
For I have not come to call the righteous, but sinners.
(vv. 12-13)

Why am I so hard on myself? Is it because my personal expectations are unrealistic? For me, midlife crises occurred at the point where my unfounded expectations collided with reality. It suddenly and dramatically dawned on me that if I were going to get "there" (wherever "there" was), I would be there by now. I simply was never going to be as great as I had secretly expected to be. My goals needed scaling downward, if I was to have any ongoing peace.

Why did my expectations overreach reality? I discovered that in part it was because I am performance-oriented. I am addicted to success and recognition. I was driving myself to achieve greater things than my parents did—especially my dad. I liked to think of myself as an innately good, morally upright person, and therefore I was forced to hide all disturbing evidence to the contrary. I discovered that I believed the lie that to be wrong is to be bad, so my unrealistic goal became never to be wrong. In the process I lost my freedom to be. Looking at the Gospels I can now see that I have just described a Pharisee. No wonder I have been so disappointed in myself!

All this time Jesus waited for me to accept my failure to achieve my own goals—my failure to recognize my wrongness, to accept myself as a sinner, and to admit that I am a weak and struggling person.

It is so easy to forget that it isn't for the healthy people that the Doctor came. It isn't the "good" people who first discover that they need Jesus. As "good" church people who look like we have it all together, we may still be offering our goodness as a sacrificial gift. But it is those of us who have fallen—who have messed up, who know that we have failed to reach our goal—who know that we need Jesus and have come to experience his mercy. Jesus is far more merciful toward us than we are toward ourselves—far more forgiving, and much less demanding. It is a relief when we accept ourselves for who we are, because we have discovered the mercy of God.

1. Are you struggling with having failed to meet your own expectations right now? Are you feeling disappointed with yourself?

2. Jesus knows all about our struggles. He accepts us, failures and all. Will you accept yourself for who you really are?

DAY TWO
What Puts Fuel in Our Tanks?

DAILY READING 1 Corinthians 13:1–13

A VERSE TO FOCUS OUR THOUGHTS
When I was a child, I talked like a child, I thought like a child,
I reasoned like a child. When I became a man,
I put childish ways behind me.
(v. 11)

It is easy to be driven by subconscious motivations learned in our childhood. Our lives become a composite of stored-away impressions. We have made numbers of decisions about who we want to be like, and who we definitely don't want to be like. We receive most of these impressions from our parents and from other significant figures from our early years.

I discovered that I had formed many of my judgments from seemingly off-handed comments my father made about people that we observed together. I remember one day when we were driving past a woman relaxing in a lawn chair in her front yard in the middle of an afternoon. Dad commented that he thought it was disgraceful to rest like that during the daytime. So then, I did too. I filed away all these comments about people, deciding that he would never catch me acting like any of them.

Childhood is filled with decisions about how we are going to be, and about what we are going to do or not do in later life. These may serve us well for a time, but more likely they will bind us in some counterproductive behavior.

Paul reminds us that it is normal to talk like children, to think like children, and to reason like children when we are young, but not after we have grown up. He encourages us to put our childish ways behind us. As we "unhook" from inappropriate childhood impressions and decisions, and from our parents' being our primary role models (or people whom we would definitely not want to be like), we can better accept Jesus as our teacher and model. I am discovering that this is a lifelong process. From time to time I have been helped by specific prayers releasing me from childish ways. As I discover more of what really motivates me, I find that I am better able to trust God with my life.

1. Did you make decisions in your earlier years that still hinder you from trusting God in current situations? Can you think of some specific ones?
2. It would help if you could talk about these with someone— a friend or perhaps a close member of your family. Often when we tell someone else we can see things more clearly ourselves.

DAY THREE
Why Not Give Up?

DAILY READING Matthew 6:5–15

A VERSE TO FOCUS OUR THOUGHTS
But we have this treasure in jars of clay
to show that this all-surpassing power is from God
and not from us.
(2 Corinthians 4:7)

When we begin to realize that we aren't who we hoped we were, when we discover that we are not going to become the persons we hoped to be, when we accept that we still have childish patterns in our adult lives—our disappointment may make it more difficult to accept ourselves. We may even come to wonder if there is any point to life at all.

Years ago I was asked to refurbish an old wrought-iron patio table for a friend. I struggled long over it and grew more and more angry at the seeming impossibility of ever making it usable again. The friend came by and, sensing my frustration, asked me what I thought of the project. In a moment of anger-fed honesty, I told him if it were my table I would throw it away. His response shocked me: "Suppose God got frustrated with you and treated you like that." I definitely got the point and the project went better—better enough that the table looked nice on his patio for years afterwards.

Praise God that he doesn't treat us the way we are tempted to treat ourselves. Sometimes I feel like throwing myself away, but he never gives up on me. He is in the restoring business and is always taking the broken pieces—the rusted furniture—and making something beautiful out of them. Just when we are tempted to despair of ever making it; that may be the moment that God is working an undetected transformation. Can we forgive ourselves for not being perfect—for failing to achieve our goals—for being weak—and accept ourselves for who we are, beloved children of a God who already knows us and is always ready to forgive us?

1. It is hard for us to admit failure, to allow for our weakness and to trust in the mercy of God. Forgiveness is a key to accepting ourselves. Will you forgive yourself?

2. Can you talk with the friend, with whom you have already shared discoveries from this devotional, about your struggles with accepting yourself?

DAY FOUR

Allowing Jesus to be Our Life

DAILY READING Romans 6:1–10

A VERSE TO FOCUS OUR THOUGHTS
I have been crucified with Christ and I no longer live,
but Christ lives in me. The life I live in the body,
I live by faith in the Son of God, who loved me and gave himself for me.
(Galatians 2:20)

Paul writes to the Colossians, "God has chosen to make known . . . the glorious riches of this mystery, which is Christ in you, the hope of glory" (1:27). Another key to accepting ourselves may be seeing that Christ lives in people like us, and therefore it is Christ who is our hope—not us. His new nature can take the place of our old nature. If we focus on our unchanging old nature we can get discouraged. In celebrating the growing new nature we can be justifiably hopeful. It is a matter of changing our focus.

To the Galatians Paul writes that our old nature died with Christ on the cross. He not only died for us, but we actually died, with him, to our old ways. Our old nature no longer needs to control us. It has died with him, and, through his rising again, he has given us a new nature. We can live a new life in Christ, because he lives again in us. That Christ would live within us is a miracle of grace—that he would transform us can be a source of unending joy.

Some time ago I was reading the familiar passage from 1 Corinthians 13, and it suddenly became a dramatic illustration to me of how Jesus becomes our life. I read, "Love is patient, love is kind . . . love does not delight in evil," etc. Subconsciously I found myself putting my name in the place of the word "love," meaning "I should be patient, I should be kind," etc., and feeling quite discouraged. I suddenly realized that Paul never intended for me to insert my name in the place of love. The Bible says that God is love, not I. Then I reread it as "God is patient," or "God in me is patient," "God in me is kind," and this passage filled me with hope as it took the burdensome "should" out of my life.

We can ask God to love people through us, giving him permission to live his life through us. That's how the transformation can take place, and Jesus can become our life.

1. Do you find yourself putting burdens on yourself—creating standards for your life that only Jesus can meet—and becoming discouraged?

2. It's much more relaxing when we are not trying to be God. Sometimes we try too hard. Jesus can show us how he wants to love people through us today.

DAY FIVE

God is Faithful and He Will Do It

DAILY READING 1 Thessalonians 5:12–24

A VERSE TO FOCUS OUR THOUGHTS
The one who calls you is faithful and he will do it.
(v. 24)

Paul showed that he understands us when he wrote these words to the Christians at Thessalonika. He was the least likely candidate to be an apostle and to become the missionary to the Gentiles. Yet God dramatically stopped him in his murderous tracks, called him, and transformed his life. When Paul refers to himself as the "chief of sinners" in his letter to Timothy, I think he truly meant those words. Paul said that God completely transformed his life.

As God called a persecuting Paul, as God called a reluctant Moses, as God redirected a runaway Jonah, as God convinced immature Jeremiahs and Timothies; so whatever our fears, our hesitations, or our unbelief, God can still fulfill his purpose in us—if we become willing.

His purpose is first that we *be* his person, that we become more like Jesus, that we be transformed by his Holy Spirit. Who we *are* is much more important than what we *do*, but he has a specific purpose for our lives, and this he is able to do. We sing in a familiar chorus:

He is able. He is able.
I know he is able.
I know my Lord is able to carry me through.

We can depend on his ability to do what he says he will do, on his faithfulness in fulfilling his every promise to us, in spite of how we feel!

Whatever he has called us to, he is "faithful and will do it." This is his promise that overrides all our unacceptable feelings about ourselves. We can be confident with Paul "that he who began a good work in you will carry it on to completion until the day of Christ Jesus" (Philippians 1:6).

1. Do you have a sense that God is asking you to do something for him?

2. If so, it could be something simple like making a phone call, or enduring another difficult day, or it might be making a life-changing decision. Will you trust God to help you?

DAY SIX

We Have a Unique Place in God's Kingdom

DAILY READING   1 Corinthians 12:12–31

A VERSE TO FOCUS OUR THOUGHTS
Now you are the body of Christ, and each one of you is a part of it.
(v. 27)

If God has placed his hand upon our lives and we belong to him, then he has something unique in mind for us. There are no duplicates in God's kingdom. Who we are, no one else can be. Our goal is to become the best that we can, at being ourselves.

All of us together form one body—the body of Christ, Paul says. This body is made up of many parts, each of which has a unique function. Each of us is asked to take her or his place. If we can accept ourselves for who we are and for what we can do, and do not look down on ourselves or our abilities, we can better take our place in the body of Christ. The better we become at being ourselves, the more valuable we are to others.

As Paul points out to the Corinthians, our jealousy of other people may cause us to devalue ourselves and withdraw. Our own narrow perspective colors our whole idea of the relative importance of members within the body of Christ. Our view of the comparative value of different functions within the body, Paul says, is skewed by our jealousy. Jealousy makes self-acceptance difficult.

We are all dependent on each other in the body of Christ. It is as if God has wired us together in series, rather than in parallel connections, like some Christmas lights. So if one light goes out, all the lights go out. This is a picture of how much we need each other. Again, we are like mountain climbers, roped together, so that when one slips, all the rest automatically become the support system.

We can measure our perspective—our feelings of worth, or lack of worth—against this picture from Corinthians. We belong because God says so. We have a unique function because God says so. God has fully accepted us as a member of his body, and therefore we can accept ourselves for who he made us to be.

1. Are you trying to be someone that God has not asked you to be? Are you struggling because you feel you have a lesser role or because you feel left out?

2. Can you hear what others may be saying to you about your gifts and abilities? It will be helpful to ask them to assist you in seeing what you have to offer, as they see it.

DAY SEVEN
Helping Others
Find Their Purpose

DAILY READING 1 Corinthians 12:1–11

A VERSE TO FOCUS OUR THOUGHTS
Now to each one the manifestation of the Spirit
is given for the common good.
(v. 7)

A s we learn to recognize ourselves as acceptable members of
the body of Christ, our goal can be to help others know
their acceptability, their belonging, their value to the whole
fellowship. Each of us brings a unique expression of Christ to
the whole group, but we often need the help of others to know
how we best fit and function. It takes other people to help us
see who we are and what our gifts are.

Paul tells us, "To each one the manifestation of the Spirit is
given for the common good" (12:7). The Holy Spirit makes
himself known differently in each one of us. This verse comes
in the context of a discussion on spiritual gifts. When we are
willing to "manifest," to "make known" the Spirit in the way he
has given us, our action becomes a gift to another member of
the body. You may be able to see things by the Spirit. These
things may seem obvious to you, but you may discover that
they are not obvious to others. When you are willing to speak,
you might give a word of encouragement or affirmation that
helps another person know what about them blesses us. You
might give a correcting word that keeps people from pursuing a
path that will not be the blessing that they hope it will.

When we are moving according to the Spirit of God, it is
helpful to have other people confirm this. I have discovered
certain abilities only after they have been pointed out to me,
because I never saw them. I wouldn't have acknowledged them

without the encouragement of others. I find myself fulfilled doing things I would not have known to choose for myself.

1. Is there someone who has blessed you just by being themselves? Could you tell them so?

2. Often we can see other people's gifts better than they can. Try to encourage someone today about what they do well. They may not be aware of their gifts.

Walking with Confidence

A VERSE FOR THE WEEK

Always giving thanks to God the Father for everything,
in the name of our Lord Jesus Christ.
(Ephesians 5:20)

What Does a Negative Attitude Look Like?

DAILY READING John 5:1–15

A VERSE TO FOCUS OUR THOUGHTS
"Sir," the invalid replied,
"I have no one to help me into the pool when the water is stirred.
While I am trying to get in, someone else goes down ahead of me."
(v. 7)

Is life an adventure, or is it more like a daily grind to endure? Do we expect good things to happen when we wake up in the morning, or do we dread most days? Do we face difficult circumstances and wonder how God is going to perform the miracle this time? Do we know with Paul that "in all things God works for the good of those who love him, who have been called according to his purpose" (Romans 8:28)? Perhaps deep inside we are protective and cautious, and would have to admit that we really believe that God is out to get us.

I can become comfortable with a generally negative attitude, having so accommodated myself to it that I am hardly aware of it anymore. It becomes my normal way of life. Negativity is in the air that we breathe in this age of cynicism and unbelief, where rallies often represent protests against, rather than support for, traditional positive values. Eeyore's hallmark observation in *Winnie the Pooh*, "It isn't much of a tail, but it's the only tail I've got," typifies the downdraft, the depressive spirit in our time.

Jesus approached a depressed invalid by the pool at Bethesda. For thirty-eight years this man had been infirm, and for a long time had been hanging around the healing waters. Jesus asked him, "Do you want to get well?" A positive answer might have been, "Yes, sir, I would love to." What we hear, however, is a long-standing complaint, a hopeless litany of frustration, paraphrased this way: "There is no one here to help me, and I can't help myself, so it is hopeless, but I'm hanging around anyway." How would we answer Jesus? Are we positive or apologetic? Is our attitude a hesitant "You wouldn't want to help me, would you?" or an expectant "Sir, I want you to heal me." The ultimate encouragement here is that Jesus cured this man in spite of his negative response.

This week we will look at how to overcome our negative outlook on life and to accept a new positive life in Jesus.

1. Do you think of yourself as spontaneous, looking on the positive side of things, or as more carefully controlled, tentative, and fearful?

2. How do you think other people see you? Would you be willing to ask someone who knows you well how she or he sees you?

DAY TWO

Negativity: What Produces It
PART ONE

DAILY READING Matthew 25:14–30

VERSES TO FOCUS OUR THOUGHTS
"Master," he said, "I knew that you are a hard man,
harvesting where you have not sown
and gathering where you have not scattered seed.
So I was afraid and went out and hid your talent in the ground.
See, here is what belongs to you."
(vv. 24-25)

Our negativity is generally systemic—a way of looking at life. It is a basic inner attitude that we have carefully cultivated for our own benefit, because we have been fearful to live a full Christian life. We may have been burned in the past and have closed in over our patterns of hurt—protecting ourselves at all costs. But the cost may be greater than we realize.

The consequence of this negativity can be most graphically seen in Jesus' parable of the talents—in the contrast between the five- and two-talent servants, and the one-talent servant. A man proportionately entrusted his property to these three servants. When they received the trust there appeared to be little difference in their attitudes. But on the day for accounting the obedient servants joyfully reported their earnings and received their reward. The third servant came forth blaming the master, defaming his character, and making him the reason for the servant's refusal to participate. The master called him "wicked" and "lazy" and had him cast into the outer darkness.

Some time ago the leader of a group with which I was meeting confronted me: He thought I was withholding my full participation and compared me to the one-talent servant. That stung, and, until I could begin to see that I was protecting myself in a dishonest way by silently accusing the leader of being too demanding. I protested vehemently. I was going to prove that life didn't have to be that difficult—I didn't have to become that vulnerable. Once I faced what I was doing, things changed much for the better.

Negativity masks itself as fear and as self-protection. As we can see from the response of the invalid at the pool and in the answer of the one-talent servant, when we are pushed we tend to accuse rather than ask for help. Using past hurt and rejection as an excuse for holding back, we refuse to jump in and fully participate.

1. Are you holding back and protecting yourself from full involvement in any present situation? Are you free to participate more fully in your Christian fellowship?

2. Can you identify any accusations with which you would want to defend yourself and that you need to admit in order to become free?

DAY THREE

Negativity: What Produces It
PART TWO

DAILY READING Psalm 32:1–10

VERSES TO FOCUS OUR THOUGHTS
When I kept silent, my bones wasted away through my groaning all day long.
For day and night your hand was heavy upon me; my strength was sapped
as in the heat of summer.
(vv. 3-4)

Another major seedbed of negativity and depression is hidden, unconfessed sin. The resultant guilt shuts us up and keeps us from being spontaneous. Sin weighs us down, causing us to withdraw and to sink into depression.

Jesus never intended for us to be able to carry the weight of our own sin. We cannot stand up under the burden of guilt. Jesus came to lift our burden, just as John Bunyan described Jesus' lifting the pack off of Pilgrim's back in *Pilgrim's Progress* and swallowing it up in the open tomb. He has rolled away our guilt so that we can become free and positive in our new life with him. However, if we bury our sin, "hiding" from God and from other people, we are denying the truth, protecting our secret, weighing down our lives, and negating God's grace.

David understood this. He had committed adultery with Bathsheba, arranged to have her faithful husband Uriah killed to cover that sin, and then married Bathsheba, all the time hoping to keep his deeds hidden in the palace. This attempt to keep his actions secret seemed to be working until God sent Nathan the prophet to confront him. To David's credit he admitted his sin, repented of it, and described his inner transformation in Psalm 32.

Before he confessed his sin he was physically wasting away inside. God's heavy hand of judgment rested upon him. His energy vanished as on the first hot day of summer. His hidden sin and deceit had depressed him and given him a totally negative spirit.

Once he admitted his sin and confessed it, he became a blessed and free man. "Blessed is he whose transgressions are forgiven, whose sins are covered . . . in whose spirit is no deceit," he shouted (Psalm 32:1-2b). God will protect him from trouble and surround him with joyous songs of deliverance. How much more positive is this scenario!

1. Ask God to show you if you have any unconfessed sin, any hidden guilt that causes you to remain burdened and depressed.

2. If something becomes obvious, would you be willing to talk about it with a wise friend?

DAY FOUR

Childlike Faith: Adults Who Are Expectant

DAILY READING   Matthew 8:5–13

A VERSE TO FOCUS OUR THOUGHTS
When Jesus heard this,
he was astonished and said to those following him, "I tell you the truth, I have not found anyone in Israel with such great faith."
(v. 10)

Have we grown up to be more childish, or more childlike? Childishness is a function of growing older without maturing. Often through trauma or other event-driven decisions, our emotional growth is arrested at various points during our formative years. Thus we can limit ourselves to childish thoughts and behavior. Childlikeness is growing up into a healthy maturity, while preserving the good qualities of a trusting, positive childhood.

I think of childlikeness as being free, spontaneous, guileless, vulnerable, expectant, and believing. Having a trustworthy human father, and transferring that trust to an even more trustworthy heavenly Father, a childlike adult would feel free to jump into God's arms at any time. This is a boldness without presumption—a positive approach without being Pollyannaish.

Perhaps it is easiest to identify such a positive attitude by looking at the example of the centurion in Capernaum. He came up to Jesus seeking healing for his paralyzed servant. He was straightforward. He made no attempt to flatter or persuade—he gave no hint of unbelief. "Just say the word, and my servant will be healed" (Matthew 8:8b). He recognized Jesus' authority. He expected people under his command to do what he said, so he expected all things on the human level to submit to the authority of Jesus. Rather than proceeding on to the centurion's house, Jesus stopped and told the centurion to go home. "It will be done just as you believed it would" (8:13b).

In faith the centurion left, knowing that his request had been granted. Why? Jesus explained, "I have not found anyone in Israel with such great faith" (8:10b). There was no question in the centurion's mind that Jesus would do this. He allowed no negativity to interfere with his request, so he could go to Jesus just as he was and recognize Jesus for who he was. Total confidence, total commitment in asking, brings results.

1. Have you approached God looking for help for yourself, or for another person, but at the same time wondered if he would give it?
2. Ask him for a gift of faith to trust him in spite of your doubts.

DAY FIVE
More Aggressive Faith

DAILY READING   Mark 2:1–12

A VERSE TO FOCUS OUR THOUGHTS
Since they could not get him to Jesus because of the crowd,
they made an opening in the roof above Jesus and, after digging through it,
lowered the mat the paralyzed man was lying on.
(v. 4.)

God honors a positive attitude—one that defies the normal expectations and proceeds through the customary human stop signs. When God asks us to do something, he does not expect us to stop doing it when we run into difficulties. What God says should override our propensity to become negative.

Imagine how the four men felt as they carried their paralyzed friend up to the house where Jesus was preaching. They had hoped to set their comrade at Jesus' feet so he could lay his hands on him and heal him, but the house was jammed with people. No amount of "excuse me's" could get them through this mob. So they rose to the challenge by carrying him up the outside stairway and dismantling the roof right over Jesus' head. What would the homeowner say? What would Jesus be thinking as the tile dust descended on him? Now here comes the man down, lowered on ropes, scattering the crowd in front of Jesus.

It doesn't say that when Jesus saw *the man*, he forgave him and healed him. It says, "When Jesus saw *their faith*," he acted (Mark 2:5a, italics mine).This was aggressive, unembarrassable, unapologetic, childlike faith. Jesus acted as if he were expecting the man. We can't embarrass Jesus.

How aggressive are we in our need? I can remember to my chagrin that as a young man I would hesitate even to run for a bus, unless I was sure I could make it, for fear of the embarrassment of having missed it. How negative! If God wanted me on that bus, I had better go for it. Threatening circumstances may challenge us but they should not stop us, if we are determined to do God's will.

1. Does the fear of embarrassment keep you from stepping out on what God has asked you to do?
2. What steps can you take to become more aggressive about your faith? Is this something you could do today?

DAY SIX
Why Do We Hang Onto Our Negativity?

DAILY READING Jonah 4:1–11

VERSES TO FOCUS OUR THOUGHTS
Jonah prayed. "Now, O Lord, take away my life,
for it is better for me to die than to live." But the Lord replied,
"Have you any right to be angry?"
(vv. 3-4)

Why do we allow negative circumstances to stop us? Why do we not push through? Why would we rather make excuses for ourselves than accept unexpected challenges? After seeing examples of aggressive faith and how Jesus honors it, even if other people consider it humanly inappropriate, can we still insist on playing safe?

These are questions that we can ask ourselves if we are in any way discouraged, downhearted, or feeling less than other people. I remember clearly hearing M. Scott Peck, a prominent psychiatrist, give this illustration: A small boy had done something wrong, and his mother punished him by sending him to his room. After an appropriate length of time she took her son's favorite dessert, a chocolate ice cream cone, up to his room and held it out to him. To her surprise, instead of eagerly taking it, he slapped his favorite dessert across the room. Dr. Peck observed that this bizarre behavior was because he was more interested in punishing his mother than he was in satisfying himself.

We often have underlying negative motives that are similarly self-defeating. High school students will underachieve and jeopardize their own academic future as a protest against their parents' control. We, too, may still be punishing a parent, or attempting to get attention at any cost, or wanting people to feel sorry for us. We may even enjoy the poor health we perpetually complain about in order to prove a point.

Jonah wanted to punish God. He had prophesied doom to the great city of Nineveh, and, surprisingly, the whole city had repented. Jonah didn't think that was fair. He didn't want his enemies spared. So, angry with God for having mercy on the "wrong people," he sat outside the city. He was angry enough to die, he said. When we want our own way rather than God's way, negativity can be the tool that we employ against him.

1. Can you see attitudes and actions in your life where you are doing things that will ultimately hurt you, because you are controlled by deeper unhealed emotions?

2. Talk about what you have seen about yourself and your deeper motives with someone who cares much for you.

DAY SEVEN
Gratitude, the Antidote

DAILY READING Luke 17:11–17

A VERSE TO FOCUS OUR THOUGHTS
Give thanks in all circumstances,
for this is God's will for you in Christ Jesus.
(1 Thessalonians 5:18)

What is the most practical way to overcome negativity and get ourselves out of the doldrums? What can we do today to change our outlook?

I suggest that we step back and try looking at our life from a wider perspective. Negativity is polarized thinking. It fastens only onto the things that are not going well, giving us a very narrow outlook. But our glass may be half full rather than half empty. If we step back we may notice that the day is actually sunny and that we are healthy, or at least healthier than a week ago. We may notice that our favorite plant has flowered.

We can find something simple for which to thank God. Then we can try to think of a second and a third thing, something that blesses us personally. This works for me. If I consciously attempt to think of positive things, I find myself thanking God that I am not where I would be if he hadn't intervened, or who I could have been if he hadn't changed me. Thanking God for Jesus and for the privilege of knowing him today, thanking him for enjoying his gift of life, will lift our spirits.

Thanksgiving or gratitude is not indigenous with us; we must work at it. Gratitude is not a natural part of our prayer life. Perhaps we will need to keep a list of things we are thankful for in order to jump-start this part of our prayer life.

In the story of Jesus' healing ten lepers, we discover that the lepers went on their way to show themselves to the priests after being healed. This was a major healing, yet only one of the ten, a Samaritan, returned to thank Jesus. Through his thanksgiving he received a greater healing. One out of ten times may be realistic for us as well. Paul reminds the Thessalonians to give thanks in *all* circumstances, because this is God's will for them.

1. Let us work at being grateful until we can find ourselves being grateful "in all circumstances." Ask God to alert you when you forget to return to him with thanksgiving.
2. Make a list of ten things that you can be grateful for right now.

Walking Together with Our Sisters and Brothers

A VERSE FOR THE WEEK
"Greater love has no one than this,
that he lay down his life for his friends."
(John 15:13)

Why We Need One Another

A VERSE TO FOCUS OUR THOUGHTS
*You also, like living stones, are being built into a spiritual house
to be a holy priesthood, offering spiritual sacrifices
acceptable to God through Jesus Christ.*
(v. 5)

Assuming that you are part of a Christian fellowship, are you learning to trust the other members of the group? Knowing other people, and allowing them to know us, enters us into the fellowship of the body of Christ.

We were not created to live alone, unless we have a special call to be a hermit. In the Garden of Eden God said, "It is not good for the man to be alone," and he created Eve to be his "helper" (Genesis 2:18). Since then, God has put us together in families so that we are automatically born into a mini-fellowship. We are created to be people of relationships. Years ago the Lone Ranger captured our imagination as a solitary hero, but he is not a good model for a Christian fellowship. Functioning alone is not desirable.

Jesus called his disciples into a fellowship with himself. The early church became a closely-knit group. Being of one accord, they owned everything in common. The letters of the New Testament were written either to churches or to leaders of churches. The images used to describe the church reveal the same thing. We are to be a human body, an integrated organism (1 Corinthians 12), and a spiritual building, an architectural unity (1 Peter 2, Ephesians 4). The emphasis is always on togetherness, as God builds us into a fellowship for his purposes.

We are quick to believe that we don't need others to help us on our spiritual journey. At the age of five I ran away from home to begin my own life, as a protest against decisions my parents were making for me. Trying to make a go of it alone as a Christian is just about that foolish. God has called us together, so that every effort we make to live out our Christian life with each other furthers God's work.

1. Are you plugged into your fellowship? Do you feel comfortable there, or are there further steps you could take to get to know people better?

2. Are you free to express your needs to your friends and to ask for their help?

DAY TWO
Bear One Another's Burdens

DAILY READING Galatians 6:1–10

VERSES TO FOCUS OUR THOUGHTS
Carry each other's burdens,
and in this way you will fulfill the law of Christ
. . . for each one should carry his own load.
(vv. 2, 5)

There is a balance between being an integral part of a fellowship and taking individual responsibility for our own spiritual lives. If we depend too much on the other members of our fellowship, we run the risk of becoming a "leaner," and this debilitating dependence will thwart our maturing as a Christian. The danger in having too much interdependence among the members is that the whole fellowship can become counterproductive and remain immature.

In the same paragraph to the Galatians, Paul writes two statements that look at first as if they contradict each other. The first is: "Each one should carry his own load" (v. 5). Each one of us is responsible to hear God for ourselves—being answerable for our own lives and direction. As we each have our own devotional practices, we become individually grounded in our personal faith. God has given to each of us "his or her own load," and he promises that he will carry it with us if we remain yoked with him.

Allegorically speaking the whole fellowship is like a large tent. Each member is represented by a tent peg, anchored in the ground. Together we secure the whole tent. We pull our own weight, but we also "carry each other's burden" (v. 2). Paul says to the Corinthians, "At the present time your plenty [money] will supply what they need, so that in turn their plenty will supply what you need" (2 Corinthians 8:14). This is also true of physical or emotional or spiritual needs.

When one is sick or incapacitated, when one is going through an emotional crisis, when one is in a faith struggle, the others who have physical, mental, or spiritual strength at the time will surround the needy person and help lift the burden. In this way we can both give and receive.

1. Are you taking responsibility for your own spiritual life? If not, you may be in danger of allowing other people to "run" your life. Jesus desires that your relationship with him take priority over your relationships with other people.

2. Are you keeping any burden to yourself, not allowing others to help lift it with you? Could you share it with at least one other person?

DAY THREE

Our Fear of Intimacy

DAILY READING Colossians 2:1–7

A VERSE TO FOCUS OUR THOUGHTS
That their hearts may be encouraged as they are knit together in love,
to have all the riches of assured understanding
and the knowledge of God's mystery, of Christ.
(v. 2 RSV)

Superficiality is a danger for a Christian fellowship. We try to sit in our pew or chair and look like the good Christian person or family, when inside we feel far different from the image we project. Being *cool* is still in vogue, and neediness is still unacceptable in Christian circles.

When my daughters were of grade-school age, I noticed that they would pass me in the church foyer and give me an exaggerated grin, but that it was gone the moment they passed me. Their grins looked so phony that I thought they were ludicrous. Then it dawned on me that my daughters were only doing what they had seen me do. I realized that what I was seeing was only a reflecting caricature, and I became convicted of "grinning" people away from me. I did this by saying "fine" with such finality when people asked me how I was doing, that they were not able to ask the more personal follow-up question. I was playing "cool" to cover my need.

A superficial fellowship is a travesty. It is like going to the doctor and never telling him or her where we hurt. Are we fearful of being known? We think that we can control what other people see of our lives. We don't want them peering through our defenses to the lonely, aching person inside. We are "little people behind the screen," like the wizard in the Wizard of Oz who was trapped within his exaggerated image, all the time wanting to cut the sham and go home.

Paul tells the Colossians that God has already "knit us together in love." He has joined us together in a loving fellowship. It is safe to allow ourselves to be known by those who share in the fellowship of Jesus, to begin to trust other people with our needs and with who we are.

1. Are you putting people off through superficial responses? The next time a friend asks you how you are doing, try to give an honest answer.

2. Is there someone hurting in your fellowship to whom you could offer your help?

DAY FOUR

Sacrificing for a Friend

DAILY READING John 15:9–17

VERSES TO FOCUS OUR THOUGHTS
My command is this: Love each other as I have loved you.
Greater love has no one than this,
that one lay down his life for his friends.
(vv. 12-13)

People are not convenient. Real relationships cannot be scheduled. Other people's needs cut across our lives, intrude into our comfort zones, and disrupt our personal plans. That's the nature of friendships. Paul challenges the Philippians: "Each of you should look not only to your own interests, but also to the interests of others" (2:4). Obviously we will look after our own interests if we are healthy. We should also look to the interests of others even, and especially, if they conflict with our own interests. True Christian fellowship is supported by sacrificial caring.

I have lived in a close Christian fellowship for over forty years now. I have discovered that living among a committed group of people automatically calls for sacrificing individual likes, desires, and plans. In spite of all the benefits, such a life is not easy. It accelerates the sanctification process, but what an energizing environment! I would not want to return to living by myself.

Jesus summarizes his commands to his disciples on their last evening together by giving them one overriding direction: "Love each other as I have loved you. Greater love has no one than this, that one lay down his life for his friends" (John 15:12b-13). Jesus ultimately died for his friends. Not many of us are called to do this, but during Jesus' life, he constantly laid down his life, preferred his disciples, and put the needs of others ahead of his own comfort. His whole life was sacrificial, and we can aspire to live as he did. In fact, he commands us to live the same way he did, and makes it possible to do so by sending us the same Holy Spirit to live his life over again in us.

1. Can you think of an occasion when you preferred yourself and decided not to put aside your plans in order to help someone else? Could you reach out to that person now?

2. Sometimes it is even more difficult to allow another person to sacrifice for you: be careful not to cheat others out of their blessing.

DAY FIVE
It is Difficult to Become Vulnerable

DAILY READING Ephesians 4:1–16

A VERSE TO FOCUS OUR THOUGHTS
Instead, speaking the truth in love,
we will in all things grow up into him
who is the Head, that is, Christ.
(v. 15)

Part of the privilege of drawing closer to other people in a Christian fellowship is learning how to become more vulnerable ourselves. We discover that we can allow other people to know us by being less selective about what we share. As we learn to open up our lives to one another we become blessed by other people's honesty and transparency.

Paul, in the context of how we are to grow up as a fellowship, tells the Ephesians that they are to "speak the truth in love." We can live in the truth together by being honest. Since we are surrounded by a deceitful society, this may take some effort on our part. Let us love one another into more and more reality about ourselves and about our relationships. Other people's perspectives on us and on our relationships may shock us from time to time. Being confronted by another person's reality can disturb us, before it sets us free.

In the Sermon on the Mount, Jesus tells the little story of the speck and the plank. He raised the question of how we can see to remove a speck of sawdust from a brother's eye if we have a whole plank in our own eye. Note, however, that having a plank does not disqualify us from helping a brother. It requires that first we need to get help removing what blocks us from seeing. Then we can help a brother remove his irritating speck. Telling people the truth, in love, helps

65

remove planks and specks and allows us to see each other more clearly. This sounds a bit risky, but Paul tells us that it is the way to "grow up."

> 1. *Living honestly with people can be threatening, but the rewards are great. Are you being dishonest in your reactions to anyone with whom you share your life? Can you go back and lovingly tell the truth?*
> 2. *Speaking in love is the key here. The longer we hold back, the harder it is to speak in love. So now is the best time to speak.*

DAY SIX
Envisioning for One Another

DAILY READING Matthew 16:13–20

A VERSE TO FOCUS OUR THOUGHTS
And I tell you that you are Peter, and on this rock I will build my church, and the gates of Hades will not overcome it.
(v. 18)

The first time that Jesus met Simon, son of John, he looked at him, and said, "You will be called Cephas," a name that is translated as Peter, and means *Rock*. Already he could see that Simon was more than a local fisherman.

Then in today's reading, Simon Peter declares that Jesus is "the Christ, the Son of the living God," and Jesus blesses him and declares, "You are Peter, and on this rock I will build my church, and the gates of Hades will not overcome it" (v. 18). Jesus envisions Peter, the impetuous, inspired spokesperson for the disciples, as the human cornerstone of his church. Jesus saw people for who they were to become.

Barnabas, the missionary partner of Paul, whose name means "Son of Encouragement," was continually helping people to be accepted for whom they were to become. He took the newly converted Saul under his wing when other Christian leaders could not see what God was doing in his life, and cared for him—advocated for him—until he could grow into "Paul." He took John Mark when Paul no longer had any use for this "quitter" and restored him to full usefulness. He was like a sculptor who could look at a block of marble and envision a fully developed person.

In a similar fashion we are given opportunities to encourage one another as God enables us to see what he is doing, or intends to do, with a member of our fellowship. Many times I have been willing—and others around me have been willing—to settle for less than what God would have for me. I am grateful for those who have encouraged me to stretch farther when I would have settled down. We are given the privilege of helping each other reach out for the best God has for us. Sometimes this will mean a gentle prod. Sometimes it will require a stronger word to keep a person from selling himself or herself short. Living up to our full potential honors Jesus and builds up his body.

1. Is there someone in your fellowship who would benefit from a word of encouragement?
2. Are you willing for God to encourage this person through you?

DAY SEVEN
Our Unity is Our Best Witness

DAILY READING John 17:20–26

A VERSE TO FOCUS OUR THOUGHTS
May they be brought to complete unity
to let the world know that you sent me
and have loved them even as you have loved me.
(v. 23b)

Jesus spoke to his disciples again, during their last evening together, saying, "All men will know that you are my disciples, if you love one another" (John 13:35). The hallmark of a Christian fellowship is love, a love for one another that is based on love for Jesus and for truth. The best way we can attract people to Jesus is by our relationships with one another. This gives the necessary validity to any word of testimony. People are starving for love and for a truly loving fellowship. They want to be included, rather than preached at. When I was in college I believed in what is known today as New Age. I had a head full of philosophical answers but was emotionally frozen and feeling alone. After a year of searching I was tentatively attracted to a Christian fellowship. Of course I thought that their beliefs were immature and their world outlook naive, but they definitely loved each other and expressed that love through caring concern, and they were willing to include me. Through this vehicle Jesus drew me to himself and to a biblical faith. Most adult converts are drawn through a genuinely loving fellowship.

Jesus envisions an even greater unity for us that will witness to the world. We overhear him praying for this when he talks with his Father. "May they be brought to complete unity to let the world know that you sent me and have loved them even as you loved me" (v. 23b). The amazing miracle is that because

Jesus came, one day we will be perfectly one through the Spirit who lives in all of us.

For now, by the same Spirit, we can work at removing anything that divides us from other Christians in our fellowship, in our church, and in the whole body of Christ. If we live honestly and truthfully so that the Spirit of Truth can do his unifying work, then Jesus will be seen among us.

1. Since unity in love is our witness, are you willing to make a priority of praying for unity in the body of Christ?
2. Are there Christians of another tradition to whom you need to reach out?

Going Forth by Faith

A VERSE FOR THE WEEK

And without faith it is impossible to please God, because
anyone who comes to him must believe that he exists
and that he rewards those who earnestly seek him.
(Hebrews 11:6)

The Opportunity for Greater Faith

DAILY READING Hebrews 11:1–12

A VERSE TO FOCUS OUR THOUGHTS
By faith Abraham,
when called to go to a place he would later receive as his inheritance,
obeyed and went, even though he did not know where he was going.
(v. 8)

Faith is a growing experience. A child's faith will not support the rigors of adulthood. Young adult faith will not be mature enough for the challenges faced by older Christians. Lack of growth in our faith walk can throw our life out of balance, and can cause spiritual deformity in the same way that lack of physical growth in a part of our body will.

We are capable of sustaining a growing faith—of having an ongoing walk with the Lord. The decision is ours. Often the challenge comes to us in the form of a major decision that confronts us. Abraham had to decide whether he was going to leave all that was familiar to him—his past, his homeland, his security—and go to an unknown place, by an unknown route, with only his faith in God to support him.

Moses, who had grown comfortable tending his father-in-law's sheep on the backside of a mountain, was confronted by a "burning bush." Would he decide to trust God's telling him that he really could deliver his people from Egypt? He had no power. He could not speak well, and he argued that out with God, but his faith was sufficient and he went.

The letter to the Hebrews gives us a whole roster of heroes of faith who obeyed because they trusted God enough to go with him into the unknown. When they had committed themselves to God they knew they had put a permanent yes on file, giving God permission to activate it whenever he chose.

If we have committed ourselves to God, then we have categorically promised to obey him.

That is part of the deal. When we are faced with a hard decision, we can trust him to expand our faith in order to encompass the unknown future, *no matter how we feel.*

1. Do you have a faith-expanding decision challenging you? Is it time to activate your yes?

2. Where do you need to put your feelings aside and trust God? Can you share this with anyone?

DAY TWO

Walking on Water

DAILY READING Matthew 14:22–33

A VERSE TO FOCUS OUR THOUGHTS
"Come," [Jesus] said. Then Peter got down out of the boat
and walked on the water to Jesus.
But when he saw the wind, he was afraid and,
beginning to sink, cried out, "Lord, save me!"
(v. 29)

Walking on water" is stereotypic for exercising expanded faith. It is the symbol of bold, if not outlandish, obedience. This expression obviously refers to Peter's walking on the water to join Jesus on the Sea of Galilee, a story full of lessons for us in our maturing faith walk.

Jesus came walking on top of the water alongside the boat in which the disciples were foundering. They became terrified. Peter asked Jesus to prove that he was their Master by inviting him to come to him on top of the water. Jesus took up his dare. Peter got out of the boat and walked almost to Jesus. Then, taking his eyes off Jesus and focusing on the wind and the waves, and beginning to sink, he panicked and cried, "Lord, save me!" Jesus did, chiding him, "You of little faith, why did you doubt?" (vv. 30b-31b).

Faith is stepping out of the boat, out of our comfort zone. It means going beyond our own safe limits in our obedience to Jesus. It involves trusting Jesus that we can do what we see him doing, as long as we continue to look to him by faith. It means keeping on in spite of contradictory circumstances.

In another context Paul encourages us: "No temptation has seized you except what is common to man. And God is faithful; he will not let you be tempted beyond what you can bear" (1 Corinthians10:13a). God knows what we can take and what we can do. In 1875 the British Parliament passed the Plimsoll Act, which required ship owners to draw a horizontal line on the bow of each ship. Then the ship could be safely loaded until this line coincided with the surface of the water. It was a safety device, but the line could not be seen from inside the ship. God keeps his eye on us, and like a watchful ship owner on the dock he knows exactly how much we can take. Most of us would draw the line much further down and become fearful far too soon. But God knows exactly how much we can each bear and how far we can go with him. His eye is upon us and he will not let us sink, we of little faith.

1. Do you think that God is asking too much of you—expecting you to do things that are beyond you?

2. Ask him to reveal to you where he has drawn his line in your life and trust him that he is carefully watching that you not be overly laden down.

DAY THREE
How Big is Our God?

DAILY READING Isaiah 6:1–8

A VERSE TO FOCUS OUR THOUGHTS
In the year that King Uzziah died, I saw the Lord seated on a throne,
high and exalted, and the train of his robe filled the temple.
(v. 1)

J.B. Phillips, an Anglican priest writing in the middle of the last century, told us in the popular little book *Your God is Too Small* that none of us has a big enough understanding of who God is. Here is the crux of our faith problem.

Isaiah was a priest, serving in the temple. One day, shortly after the king had died—the throne was empty—Isaiah was going about his daily duties when suddenly a veil was drawn back and he entered a whole new realm. The Lord himself was sitting on the emptied throne and his presence and entourage filled the whole temple. Isaiah was totally awed, overcome with a sense of God's holiness and his own unworthiness. How could he not say yes to a God like this?

John was on the Island of Patmos worshiping on the Lord's Day when suddenly he was captured by the overwhelming presence of the glorified Jesus. John turned to look at him, and the impact forced him to the ground. How could he not say yes to an invitation from such a one as this? The result is the book of Revelation.

Elisha and his servant were surrounded by the enemy forces of Israel, and the servant panicked. Elisha asked God to open his servant's eyes to what he himself could see. As if he had put on special glasses, the servant could now see a whole new world. The surrounding hills were filled with horses and chariots of fire, the Lord's superior army (2 Kings 6).

I clearly remember running down the East Lake Road of Canandaigua Lake in Western New York State one night when

I was faced with a major faith decision. I was running away from it, and from God. I sat down on a cement culvert, all alone, until I "chanced" to look up. There, over my head, was a convergence of great lights forming a gigantic cathedral dome that filled the sky. I was struck with the immensity of God. I knew that I could never run far enough to get away from this God. So I made a life-changing decision to follow him.

1. Read Isaiah 40:21–31. Measure the God that you prayed to this morning by Isaiah's view of who God is.
2. Ask God to reveal himself to you—to roll back the veil— so that you can glimpse the spiritual world that surrounds you.

DAY FOUR
What Hinders Our Maturing in Faith?

DAILY READING Matthew 6:5–15

A VERSE TO FOCUS OUR THOUGHTS
Our Father in heaven, hallowed be your name, your kingdom come,
your will be done on earth as it is in heaven.
(v. 9b)

Yesterday we were looking at our understanding of God, seeing how small it may be and asking God to reveal himself to us again. Today we will look at other ways in which our view of God is skewed. We may be overly afraid of God because we haven't discovered how merciful he is. As a result we may relate to him as little as possible. On the other hand, we may tend to think of God as a giant pal who requires little faith on our part.

When we pray, whom do we address? Are we more comfortable praying to our heavenly Father, or do we pray mostly to Jesus, or even to the Holy Spirit? Sometimes we aren't even aware who we are addressing until we consciously stop and listen to ourselves. I suspect that we pray to the one with whom we are the most comfortable. If we find that we pray to Jesus only, we probably do so because our view of God is still inextricably entangled with our view of our human father. Such exclusive prayer may indicate that we still have some forgiving to do and some mercy to discover. If we pray only to God the Father, our doing so may show that we are still fearful of an intimate relationship with God, and this, too, may be because of our past hurtful experiences of intimacy.

If we are not comfortable with the Father or with Jesus, we are blocked from fully trusting God. Our faith is at least partly in ourselves, and it will fail us in a time of need.

Jesus in the Sermon on the Mount constantly refers to God as "your Father." He teaches us to address God as "our Father." Over and over again he encourages us to trust him unconditionally—not to worry, but to have greater faith in him. Do we trust God? If not, Jesus says we can. He found his Father totally trustworthy. We can trust him just like Jesus did and join in Jesus' faith.

1. It's okay to discover that you are uncomfortable with a member of the Trinity. He understands. You can talk with him about this.

2. Is your relationship with your father, or some other influential person in your life, keeping you from fully trusting God as your loving heavenly Father—from knowing deep inside that he cares for you? Ask God to help you with this relationship.

DAY FIVE

Standing on the Promises of Victory

DAILY READING John 17:6–12

A VERSE TO FOCUS OUR THOUGHTS
For I gave them the words you gave me and they accepted them.
(v. 8a)

If we trust God we should take him at his word. In fact, he tells us that we can use his words. These words continue his authority. We can step out in faith in his name and declare his victory in situations in our life today.

This is an interesting phrase in Jesus' prayer to his Father: "For I gave them the words you gave me and they accepted them." When the Holy Spirit came at Pentecost the disciples discovered a new boldness when they proclaimed the words that Jesus had given them.

Jesus defeated Satan during his temptation by quoting his Father's words recorded in the Old Testament. Each time he began, "It is written. . . ." When we are under spiritual attack—when we are harassed or feeling hopeless—we have Jesus' words at our disposal and we can boldly declare them. Jesus said on the cross, "It is finished" (John 19:30), meaning that salvation is complete and Satan and death are defeated. John expands on this truth: "The reason the Son of God appeared was to destroy the devil's work" (1 John 3:8). Therefore he is defeated, and we can declare that fact in our present difficulty. Isaiah tells us, "By his wounds we are healed" (53:5c). If we believe this and similar Scriptures, we can have the authority—the faith—to declare healing in his name.

Paul tells the Ephesians about our spiritual armor for our battle. Note that the only offensive weapon we have is "the sword of the Spirit, which is the word of God" (6:17b), because that is all we need. We can wield the word like a sword to defeat the enemy and proclaim the victory of Jesus over sickness, harassment, and temptation. Let us exercise our faith and stand on his word.

1. Memorize three Scriptures that declare Jesus' victory and have them available to use like a spiritual sword.
2. Next time you pray for someone, remember that you can be bold in claiming scriptural promises for them.

DAY SIX

Standing on the Promises of Comfort

DAILY READING Isaiah 43:1–21

VERSES TO FOCUS OUR THOUGHTS
"When you pass through the waters, I will be with you;
and when you pass through the rivers, they will not sweep over you . . .
for I am the Lord, your God, the Holy One of Israel, your Savior."
(vv. 2a-3a)

God's word is full of promises that we can claim. God delights to have us open the Bible and point to something he has said—some promise he has given us—and ask him to fulfill it here and now. He wants us to believe like Abraham, who Paul describes in Romans as "being fully persuaded that God had power to do what he had promised" (4:21). We can take God at his word. Oh, that we *would* take God at his word!

Again it is good to memorize several key promises that can give us comfort and confidence during times of stress. My favorite verse is Isaiah 30:15b, "In repentance and rest is your salvation, in quietness and trust is your strength." Jesus makes this promise: "Come to me, all you who are weary and burdened, and I will give you rest" (Matthew 11:28). The writer to the Hebrews quotes God's promise: "Never will I leave you; never will I forsake you" (13:5b). Again in this week's passage from Isaiah we read, "When you pass through the waters, I will be with you; when you pass through the rivers, they will not sweep over you . . . for I am the Lord, your God." These are promises in which we can trust.

Can we throw away all our self-protective devices and save all the energy that we put into taking care of ourselves, because God has promised us over and over again that he will take care of us? We will go through difficulties—deep water—but we will not drown. We will be tempted to doubt, but he will not fail us. If we believe this, our anxiety level can be greatly reduced, and our faith just might move mountains—the obstacles in our path.

1. Are you facing a difficult situation? Take one of the promises from this devotional, or another one that you prefer, and ask God to make it real for you.

2. Is someone close to you going through a difficult time? Ask God to give you a promise for that person and then give it, or send it, to her or to him as a gift.

DAY SEVEN
The Rewards of Faith

DAILY READING Genesis 15:1–21

A VERSE TO FOCUS OUR THOUGHTS
After this the word of the Lord came to Abram in a vision:
"Do not be afraid, Abram. I am your shield, your very great reward."
(v. 1)

When we exercise our faith, God rewards us. The Bible makes many references to rewards. They are a common theme in Jesus' parables. Heaven is a reward for faith. More accurately, God himself is our reward. By taking steps of faith we gain God through Jesus. Humanly speaking, spiritual rewards are contingent upon our faith.

When we initially place our faith in Jesus, our reward is eternal life (John 6:40). We are assured of our salvation and of a future life in heaven. We gain access to grace for our daily Christian lives as a reward for our faith (Romans 5:2). We must continue this faith walk, being obedient to all of God's directives, if we are to continue to receive the "great reward" that David talked about in Psalm 19:11.

Abraham is the classic example of a man who walked by faith. For twenty-three years he believed that God would one day fulfill his promise to give him a natural son. From time to time Abram's faith would waver and God would have to renew his promise, but then Abram would again believe God, and God "credited it to him as righteousness" (Genesis15:6).

Like Abraham we must daily walk by active faith. This is the only way to maintain our confidence in Jesus. It is the only way to be bold to step out on the promises of God. It is the only way to have peace with God (Romans 5:1). These are our ongoing spiritual rewards in this life.

Not long ago I was asked to change jobs, at a time in my life when I felt that change was inappropriate. I was told that the change would become a blessing for me if I stayed with it. I reluctantly took people's word, but I had a difficult transition. But after several weeks I began to see the truth of what was said and began to believe it for myself. Perhaps you, like me, have fought many suggested changes in your life and have made them under initial protest, only to discover that they were the doorways to your greatest blessings. I have found again that God rewards those who continue to trust him in spite of how they feel.

1. Are you balking at making a suggested change in your life? This could be a major move or it could be a private matter of preferring another person. Read the references included in this devotional if you haven't already.

2. Would you be willing to move forward on faith and trust God for the promised rewards?

The Lonely Road of Suffering

A VERSE FOR THE WEEK
And the God of all grace, who called you to his eternal
glory in Christ, after you have suffered a little while,
will himself restore you
and make you strong, firm and steadfast.
(1 Peter 5:10)

Suffering
is Not Our Favorite Thing

DAILY READING 1 Peter 4:12–19

A VERSE TO FOCUS OUR THOUGHTS
Dear friends, do not be surprised at the painful trial you are suffering,
as though something strange were happening to you.
(v. 12)

No one naturally wants to suffer. Instinctively we recoil from suffering, because it has not become a friend. We may feel sorry for ourselves when we are in pain, and we may think of our suffering as punishment and quietly wonder what we did to deserve it. We all have our fears of specific forms of suffering. As a child I sat by and watched my uncle slowly lose his eyesight, so I grew up overly afraid of going blind myself.

Does God see suffering the same way we do? Have we accepted the world's view of pain? Comfort and ease are the goals offered by the advertising industry. We are constantly being told that life should be easy, relaxing, and without conflict, and we are encouraged to try the latest remedy guaranteed to ease our physical or emotional pain. This is the world's perspective. Can we expect the world to understand suffering from a Christian point of view?

The Bible has a more realistic understanding of suffering. Early Christians knew the redemptive value of pain. For a time in Christian history martyrdom was an aspiration because it was the supreme way to testify for Jesus—to "endure hardship like a good soldier of Christ Jesus" (2 Timothy 2:3). We are not advocating martyrdom, but we are suggesting that how we understand and handle our pain can testify to our faith.

Peter encouraged people who were in pain not to be surprised by it, as if it were something unusual. It is the normal expectation for a committed Christian, because through it we come to share with Christ in a deeper way.

This week we hope to come to a better understanding of how suffering can be our friend.

1. Are you struggling with a physical or emotional affliction, or some place of continual discomfort?

2. Ask God to show you how he views your pain. He can help you understand the redemptive value of it.

DAY TWO

Accepting Pain as a Part of a Christian's Life

DAILY READING Hebrews 12:4–13

VERSES TO FOCUS OUR THOUGHTS
And have you forgotten that word of encouragement
that addresses you as sons: "My son, do not make light of the Lord's discipline,
and do not lose heart when he rebukes you,
because the Lord disciplines those he loves."
(vv. 5-6a)

Pain is part of the human experience. We can attempt to deny it—we can live above it; we can try to live around it; but it is still a fact of life. So as Christians, let us try to live with it and to have God show us its value in our lives.

The writer to the Hebrews suggests that discipline is painful. Surprisingly, he says that this is a sign of our heavenly Father's love. How can this be? "He punishes everyone he accepts as a son" (12:6b). Suffering has a purpose in God's plan. It is one of his best encouragements to cause us to grow in our faith.

God led Abraham through a painful experience when he instructed him to sacrifice his only son, Isaac. God allowed

Joseph to endure many painful years of slavery and imprisonment to prepare him for his role in saving his people. Job experienced grave hardships after God gave permission for him to be severely harassed. But the greatest example is what happened to God's own Son in order to secure our salvation. As we stand in awe before the cross we can understand suffering a lot better. Even though he was God, Jesus learned much through what he suffered. Down through the centuries God's people have suffered and matured.

Teresa of Avila, a sixteenth-century saint, made a famous reflection during a time of personal suffering: "If this is the way you treat your friends, it is no wonder that you have so few of them." God treats his friends "this way" because he loves us and knows what is better for us. He is willing to be misunderstood, to be seen as unloving and unmerciful, until we too can see the value of our suffering.

Jesus realistically prepared his disciples for the Christian life. "In this world you will have trouble. But take heart! I have overcome the world" (John 16:33). He does not take us out of our situations, he takes us *through* them. Can we trust him?

1. Think back to when you were disciplined as a child, or when you disciplined your children. Can you see good coming from the experience?
2. In your adult experience can you see instances when God has used your trouble to "discipline" you as his child?

DAY   THREE
Seeing God's Greater Purpose in our Suffering

DAILY READING 1 Peter 1:3–9

VERSES TO FOCUS OUR THOUGHTS
In this you greatly rejoice, though now for a little while you may have had
to suffer grief in all kinds of trials. These have come so that your faith—
of greater worth than gold, which perishes even though refined by fire—
may be proved genuine.
(vv. 6-7a)

We have seen that suffering is not to be considered a random or accidental experience. In other words, God is not caught by surprise by what we are going through. There is a divine purpose in suffering. This is not to suggest that God is the author of all suffering, but it is certainly one way that he draws us closer to himself. Will we cooperate with him and allow this to happen?

Through our suffering either we can become softer, more vulnerable, and more available to God's love, or we can become more isolated, bitter and angry. In either case suffering gets our attention.

Peter challenges us to accept trials as a testing of our faith— as a purifying process. Our faith is more precious than gold, in God's sight. Jesus teaches us that our faith relationship with him is "the pearl of great value"(Matthew 13:46). Pearls are formed within an oyster because an irritant has intruded. Our lives become of greater value because we have allowed an intruding irritant to draw us closer to Jesus. He is able to create something more beautiful because of it. Perishable gold is refined by fire to remove the dross. Our imperishable souls are purified by the pressure of trials so that our faith becomes stronger and more able to endure.

Can we see our suffering from the long view—what it is preparing us for? Paul tells the Corinthians that even though their bodies may be wasting away through physical difficulties, inwardly they were being renewed every day. Often these two seemingly contradictory processes go on simultaneously. From the perspective of eternity, Paul says, the hardships are "light and momentary" compared to the eternal glory that far outweighs them all. Suffering may be preparing us for the far greater things ahead.

1. Do you have an idea of what God is preparing you for? Perhaps he would allow you a glimpse of it so that you can better see the circumstances in your life in the context of the future.
2. Ask him especially to show you how your present situation is drawing you closer to him.

DAY FOUR

Allowing Our Pain to Work for Us

DAILY READING   Isaiah 52:13–53:12

A VERSE TO FOCUS OUR THOUGHTS
But he was pierced for our transgressions, he was crushed for our iniquities;
the punishment that brought us peace was upon him,
and by his wounds we are healed.
(v. 53:5)

Most of us are suffering in one way or another, but is our suffering redemptive? This is the crucial question. As we saw yesterday, suffering can be either the means by which we are drawing closer to God or the ground for building a stronger case against him. The same sun that shines on wax and softens it, shines on clay and hardens it. Let us hope that we are becoming more pliable in God's hands.

Since we all experience pain, the deciding question is whether or not we will allow it to work for us. A close friend of mine underwent double knee replacement surgery this past week. This seemed like a bold move, but since her knees hurt so badly, she decided to have both surgeries at the same time. To her—and her friends'—amazement she discovered that she felt less pain after the surgery than before it. She had suffered for years, and her knees had just gotten worse. Her previous suffering was doing no good. So she was happy with her post-operative pain, because it was pain that was leading to healing. It was redemptive pain—the pain of recovery. She is already walking again.

When we take our pain to the great physician, he transforms it from enduring pain to healing pain—pain that allows us to walk again by faith. When we know that God is healing us and redeeming us, then the pain will no longer be our focus.

The writer to the Hebrews describes Jesus as "the author and perfecter of our faith, who for the joy set before him endured the cross, scorning its shame, and sat down at the right hand of the throne of God" (12:2). Jesus kept the ultimate goal in view and saw his pain within the greater framework of joy. His suffering as Isaiah enumerated it (chapters 52-53) was totally redemptive. Suffering brought us salvation, healing, deliverance, and eternal life. Suffering drew him to his Father and to his greater purposes. He never allowed it to separate him from his Father. He never had to "guts it through" with gritted teeth. He always kept his suffering in perspective. And he can help us to do this as well.

1. God has set joy before us as it was set before Jesus. Ask him to remind you of this joy in practical ways.
2. Sometimes thanksgiving can help put a joyful framework back into our lives. List five things that you are grateful for today.

DAY FIVE

God's Power is Made Perfect in Our Weakness

DAILY READING 2 Corinthians 12:1–10

A VERSE TO FOCUS OUR THOUGHTS
My grace is sufficient for you, for my power is made perfect in weakness.
(v. 9a)

Not only does God call us to go through difficult times and to endure hardships, but also he promises to go through them with us. He is there in the midst of our pain. He has sent the Holy Spirit to live within us and to be our Comforter. God has promised us, "When you pass through the waters, I will be with you" (Isaiah 43:2).

Paul reminds us, "God is faithful; he will not let you be tempted beyond what you can bear. But when you are tempted, he will also provide a way out so that you can stand up under it" (1 Corinthians 10:13). He knows better than we do how much we can take. Can we trust him when we have a difference of opinion?

When Paul was suffering he pleaded with God three times to take away his source of pain, his "thorn in my flesh" (2 Corinthians 12:7). He told God just how he felt about it. Contrary to our expectations, God did not remove the thorn for this faithful apostle, but rather he told him the greater purpose for it. His suffering kept his life in balance while he was receiving so many revelations. Paul discovered the redemptive value of his suffering and submitted to God's better plan. He accepted his thorn and learned to "delight in weaknesses, in insults, in hardships, in persecutions, in difficulties" (v. 10). God promises that his grace is sufficient for us (v. 9a). He is with us; he will see us through. "For my power is made perfect in weakness" (v. 9b RSV).

Not long ago I was plagued with insomnia. For months I awoke around four each morning, feeling angry, anxious, and in turmoil. Day after day I pleaded with God to allow me to sleep. Then one day he showed me that I was refusing his gift. He wanted me to use this private time to be with him, and when I did, those dreaded times were turned into special moments of fellowship with him.

1. Do you have a "thorn" that you haven't talked with God about? His perspective on it may give you a new appreciation for his better way.

2. Can you recall a time when God turned a frustrating problem in which you saw no value into a great blessing for you?

DAY SIX

The Transforming Power of Suffering

DAILY READING Genesis 50:15–21

VERSES TO FOCUS OUR THOUGHTS
But Joseph said to them, "Don't be afraid. Am I in the place of God?
You intended to harm me, but God intended it for good
to accomplish what is now being done, the saving of many lives."
(vv. 19-20)

We have a common expression, "No pain, no gain." But it is true that the deeper changes in our lives often involve some suffering. Jesus described himself as a "kernel of wheat" that "falls into the ground and dies" (John 12:24). It takes the death of the seed to produce fruit. It takes the sacrifice of the caterpillar to produce a butterfly. It took the death of Jesus to produce the body of Christ. "In bringing many sons to glory, it was fitting that God . . . should make the author of their salvation perfect through suffering" (Hebrews 2:10).

Joseph, who was a prototype of Jesus, was a dreamer as a teenager, without much wisdom. One day, when he approached his jealous brothers in a distant field, they acted out their feelings by throwing him into a deep cistern. Then they changed their minds and sold him as a slave to a caravan of Ishmaelites traveling to Egypt. Later on he spent years languishing in an Egyptian prison as the result of trumped-up charges. But through supernatural circumstances he was elevated to become second in command of the whole country. From this position he saved many lives, including those of his father Jacob and the brothers who had sold him. He was now full of both wisdom and common sense. Through his trials he came to know God and his purposes, and was enabled to see God's greater plan in all that had befallen him. Thus he was prepared to forgive his guilty brothers. This amazing transformation came through suffering.

I know a young man who a year ago wished to die. He was already emotionally "dead," and his life had turned a hopeless shade of gray. It was then that he discovered that he had life-threatening cancer and that the prognosis was grim. Following surgery he submitted to months of chemotherapy and radiation treatments. He also received much spiritual counseling, and today he is a vibrant, energetic, hope-filled, cancer-free Christian, transformed by God through what he suffered.

1. Do you have a story to tell of how God used adversity or suffering in your life to bring about a transformation? Share this with a friend.

2. Think of a person who is facing difficulties in his or her life. Pray that they would receive the full benefit for this experience.

DAY SEVEN
The Mystery of Suffering

DAILY READING Hebrews 12:4–13

A VERSE TO FOCUS OUR THOUGHTS
No discipline seems pleasant at the time, but painful.
Later on, however, it produces a harvest of righteousness and peace
for those who have been trained by it.
(v. 11)

Having considered this week the subject of suffering, we still discover that it is a mystery. We want to be able to explain everything, to understand it and to be in control of it, but how God uses our suffering remains a mystery to us. Eliphaz told Job, "[God] performs wonders that cannot be fathomed, miracles that cannot be counted" (Job 5:9). Suffering is one of these wonders.

Jesus' coming as a human being is a mystery. Even though he revealed much about his relationship with his Father, that relationship still is beyond our understanding. That God would make Jesus perfect through suffering (Hebrews 2:10) boggles our mind. How we share in his suffering, and are likewise sanctified through it, remains a mystery as well.

Paul suffered many hardships. God told Ananias that Paul was his chosen instrument to carry his name before the Gentiles and their kings, and revealed to Ananias that "I will show him how much he must suffer for my name" (Acts 9:16). Paul's own testimony was that "we who are alive are always being given over to death for Jesus' sake, so that his life may be revealed in our mortal body" (2 Corinthians 4:11). Because Paul was willing to suffer, the testimony of Jesus became known throughout the Roman Empire.

In 1990, when Russia was still under communist rule, I had the privilege of attending an evening service at the Moscow Baptist Church. I sat in the balcony and looked into the faces of the *babushkas*, the older women, sitting in the balcony opposite me. The years of oppression, the loss of family members, their suffering for their faithfulness to Jesus—these were deeply etched in their beautiful faces. What happened to them had mysteriously changed them—transformed them as nothing else could have done As I watched, a Russian soldier in dress uniform went forward to receive Christ that night. I knew that there was a connection between his bold public move and the years of suffering represented in the balcony.

1. My grandmother suffered much for her faith, but during those years she prayed much for me because I didn't know Christ. I know that my coming to faith was the fruit of her faithfulness. Is your life in Christ the fruit of someone else's suffering?
2. Are you willing to continue in your difficulties, trusting in God's mysterious ways to bring good from it for others?

Learning to Wait for God

I wait for the Lord, my soul waits,
and in his word I put my hope.
My soul waits for the Lord
more than watchmen wait for the morning,
more than watchmen wait for the morning.
(Psalm 130:5-6)

We Live in a Restless Society

DAILY READING Ecclesiastes 2:17–26

VERSES TO FOCUS OUR THOUGHTS
What does a man get for all the toil and anxious striving
with which he labors under the sun? All his days his work is pain and grief;
even at night his mind does not rest. This too is meaningless.
(vv. 22-23)

A word that captures the essence of our society is *speed*. We continually attempt to do things faster and more efficiently. Our attention span becomes shorter. Our need for constant stimulation is greater. Communication is now instantaneous. We have come to expect things to happen immediately. What a change from the experience of past generations!

Think about how differently our children are being raised today—on a succession of one-second long television images, on instant cell-phone communication with anyone in the world, on high-speed Internet connections that can provide immediate information on any subject. What will their adult lives be like? Patience has become a lesser virtue, and therefore is more difficult to learn and maintain.

We have become people of instant gratification. A friend of mine jokingly referred to "roughing it" as having to tolerate slow room service. A generation ago that might have been funnier. The prophetic word of Lewis Carroll in *Alice in Wonderland* is being lived before us. The Red Queen had Alice by the hand, dragging her along at breakneck speed, yelling "faster, faster." When Alice complained, the Queen responded, "We have to go this fast just to stand still."

The Teacher in Ecclesiastes refers to this as "chasing after the wind" (2:17, 26). He raises the question as to where all this anxious striving gets us. Ecclesiastes was written to prove the fruitlessness of our worldly culture.

Over and against all of this can we learn to live according to God's ways, to wait upon him, to trust him to see us through in his time. This is a major challenge for us post-modern people— a challenge we will be encouraged to accept during the week ahead. Let us not be falsely energized by the culture we live in. Let us learn to wait upon the Lord!

1. Are you caught up in the swirl of the life surrounding you? Can you hear God leading you to slow down so that you can walk with him?

2. Are there specific ways that you are already aware of, in which you need to slow down the pace of your life?

DAY TWO

The Restlessness Within Us

DAILY READING Isaiah 57:14–21

A VERSE TO FOCUS OUR THOUGHTS
But the wicked are like the tossing sea, which cannot rest,
whose waves cast up mire and mud.
(v. 20)

Waiting upon the Lord is made more difficult by the fact that restlessness is not only around us, but also within us. Waiting and "wasting time" are naturally anathema to the Western work ethic, and we are in tune with our society by nature. Our own schedules are automatically more important to us than anyone else's. Slow drivers annoy us. People chatting with the cashier on the checkout line are inconsiderate, because they are in our way. Our inner motors are revved up by nature and by training.

As long as I am under the pressure to produce I feel that I have an excuse for my impatience. When my life is suddenly, and miraculously, free of deadlines, I am surprised to discover that I am still anxious. So I find myself creating artificial deadlines in order to justify this continued tension. This is an easier alternative than attempting to slow down and face my anxiety.

It should be no surprise, then, that Isaiah reminds us that sinful natures are like the tossing sea, which cannot rest. Its waves are always stirring things up—muddying situations. True peace can come only from God. Our constant attempts to create our own sense of well-being by speeding past our problems, will prove futile. Patience is a derivative of a peace that is not ours to create. Once we understand this, we can turn to God rather than strive on in our own strength.

Augustine's famous quote is that "our souls are restless until they find their rest in thee." Only God can give us true peace, true rest, and a slower mind. Only he can give us a patient heart.

1. Are you willing to ask God to help you slow down? Can you give your anxieties, your circumstances, your frustrations over to him?

2. Can you place your daily schedule in God's hands and let him help you with your priorities, so that you will have more time for him?

DAY THREE
Being Patient with God

DAILY READING Psalm 37:1–13

VERSES TO FOCUS OUR THOUGHTS
Be still before the Lord and wait patiently for him;
do not fret when men succeed in their ways,
when they carry out their wicked schemes.
(v. 7)

Scripture is full of directives such as "Be still, and know that I am God" (Psalm 46:10) and "Wait patiently for him" (Psalm 37:7). The implication here is that God's timetable and ours may not be the same. God often appears to us as the slow motorist on the road or the chatty person in the checkout line. We may discover that much of our praying is an attempt to get God to be as urgently concerned about things as we are. We want him to rev up to our speed, rather than for us to slow down and to trust him.

Jesus moved at his Father's pace. At a time when it seemed most urgent for him to go quickly to Bethany in order to save Lazarus' life, he, to the disciples' dismay, waited for an additional two days before going. At another time the disciples were insistent that Jesus come back into Capernaum to heal all those gathered there, yet Jesus, after waiting on his Father, went on to the other villages of Galilee. God's timing is more important than the demands of the urgent.

David instructs us not to be concerned about God's timetable with other people either, especially those we see doing 'bad' things. James and John, the Sons of Thunder, wanted to call down fire on the Samaritan villages that would not allow them to pass through on their way to Jerusalem, but Jesus rebuked them for their impatience. Other people, and the consequences of their behavior, are God's business. Staying in constant touch with him is the only way not to get ahead of his schedule.

In the words of an old hymn by Bradford Torrey:

Not so in haste, my heart! Have faith in God and wait;
Although he linger long, He never comes too late.

He never cometh late; He knoweth what is best;
Vex not thyself in vain; Until he cometh, rest.

1. Will you remain quietly before God long enough to hear his still, small voice telling you to give him your burden and to wait for him to act?
2. Do you feel that God is unfair by allowing another person to get away with too much or to do things that you cannot do? That is a heavy burden that leads to restlessness. Can you give that over to God as well?

104

DAY FOUR

Being Patient with Other People

DAILY READING Ephesians 4:25–5:2

A VERSE TO FOCUS OUR THOUGHTS
Be kind and compassionate to one another, forgiving each other,
just as in Christ God forgave you.
(v. 32)

We may transfer the demands that we make upon God to other people and expect them to jump to meet our requests. To the extent that we think of God as a divine genie who should be prepared to respond to our every wish, we will consider other people as an extension of this need-meeting requirement.

Mary had learned how to wait upon God. She was sitting at Jesus' feet when her sister, Martha, came bursting forth from the kitchen. Rather than addressing her sister directly, Martha turned to Jesus in her impatience and demanded that he make Mary help her. Martha was upset and out of touch with what God was doing, and was taking her anger out on her sister. How often is our impatience acted out against someone else? Jesus wasn't so concerned with the preparations being made for his visit as he was with Martha's self-centered attitude. When she could see things from his viewpoint, she would be at peace with what Mary was doing.

Being at peace with God, and content with his schedule, is the first step in caring for other people, especially for our sisters and brothers in Christ. If we are at peace with God and his schedule, we discover that other people are not such a large problem.

We can respond to Paul's encouragement to "be kind and compassionate to one another" (Ephesians 4:32). We can be merciful and slow to anger because "love is patient" (1 Corinthians 13:4). When someone wrongs us, rather than condemn them, punish them, or get irritated with them, we can forgive them (whether or not they admit they are wrong). Of course we will continue to get hurt. Of course we will continue to hurt others as well. Let us not be surprised that this happens again and again. It is not our goal to change other people. God said that this was his business, and it is on his timetable. Our goal is to forgive them.

1. Is there anyone you would like to change right now? Can you pray for that person, asking God to show you how he feels about her or him?

2. Is there someone else with whom you are impatient? Ask God to show you why. Often this person is more of a reflection of us than we would like to admit.

DAY FIVE

Being Patient with Ourselves

DAILY READING Micah 7:18–20

A VERSE TO FOCUS OUR THOUGHTS
You will again have compassion on us; you will tread our sins underfoot
and hurl all our iniquities into the depths of the sea.
(v. 19)

Although we get impatient with God and with some of his other children, the one we are most often impatient with is ourselves. In other words, we expect more from ourselves than we ought to expect. "By this age I ought to be more mature than this." "Why do I increasingly forget why I just came upstairs?" "What makes me continually do the thing that irritates my spouse?" "Why do I continue to cheat on my diet?" These questions become more frequent and more worrisome as we get older.

Some of us have spent years learning and reinforcing poor habit patterns. We are not apt to change quickly, unless God miraculously shortens the process. These twelve weeks of study are a good start, but let's be patient with ourselves while we are reprogramming well-worn circuits in the brain.

We are also getting older, and certain things become more difficult to do. This requires more patience. Forgetting things does not telegraph the onset of Alzheimer's disease, but it does necessitate an adjustment for proud people.

I remember well hearing Corrie ten Boom, an author and speaker who knew the love of the Father say, as a paraphrase of today's passage in Micah, "God tosses all our sins into the depths of the sea, and then puts up a little sign which reads 'No fishing.'" Being patient with ourselves means we need to become more like God and "delight to show mercy" to ourselves. Rather than staying angry with ourselves, we can learn to forgive ourselves more quickly, and then, like God, to forget about it and no longer fish around in that area. Let us allow ourselves to be human.

1. Are you still "nurdling" about some mistake you have made or some situation you fouled up? Can you forgive yourself and stop "fishing"?

2. It is okay to forget something without always fretting about losing your memory. The next time you forget something, quickly forgive yourself.

DAY SIX

Impatience Can Be Costly

DAILY READING Genesis 16:1–16

A VERSE TO FOCUS OUR THOUGHTS

He will be a wild donkey of a man; his hand will be against everyone and everyone's hand against him, and he will live in hostility toward all his brothers.

(v. 12)

God promised Abram that he would become a great nation, but Abram was seventy-five years old and had no children.

So he inquired of the Lord, who specifically promised him "a son coming from your own body" (Genesis 15:4). After another ten years of waiting, Abram and Sarai decided to take matters into their own hands and help fulfill what God had promised them. Sarai offered her handmaiden Hagar to Abram, and he had a son by her and named him Ishmael. It was another thirteen years before their own son Isaac was born. Only then was God's promise fulfilled.

What about Ishmael? He was the fruit of impatience and was hardly to be a peaceful influence in the world. The angel of the LORD said he would be "a wild donkey of a man . . . and he will live in hostility toward all his brothers" (16:12). His descendants were always antagonistic to Isaac's descendants. The tragic history of unrest in the Middle East can be traced to Abram and Sarai's impatience. Here is a vivid demonstration of the consequence of moving ahead of God.

Impatience is often expressed in impetuousness. Esau, because he was temporarily famished, was willing to sacrifice his birthright to Isaac (Genesis 25:33). Moses moved impulsively at Kadesh and God kept him from entering the Promised Land (Numbers 20). King Saul did not wait for Samuel, but moved rashly and disobediently ahead in offering up the burnt offering, and God removed his kingship (1 Samuel 13). These are some drastic scriptural examples of costly impatience.

The fruit of impatience is disobedience. How often do the impatient demands of our bodies, our emotions, or our minds lead us into disobedience? How often do we sacrifice God's long-range plans in order to meet immediate needs? Impatience can result in substance abuse, sexual infidelity, indebtedness, and broken families; but always it results in the loss of inner peace. We can see again that it is important that we do God's will in God's time.

1. Have you become impatient and tried to make something happen, only to discover that you had actually messed things up?

2. *What did your impatience cost you? This would be a helpful thing to journal about.*

DAY SEVEN

The Fruit of Patience

DAILY READING Psalm 40:1–17

A VERSE TO FOCUS OUR THOUGHTS
He lifted me out of the slimy pit, out of the mud and mire;
he set my feet on a rock and gave me a firm place to stand.
(v. 2)

Patience waits on God each step of the way. Being patient means being constantly alert to the moving of the Holy Spirit in our lives. Patience requires standing on what God has said regardless of what other people think or of what we fear it will cost us.

David said that he "waited patiently for the LORD" (Psalm 40:1a). For thirteen years he waited after Samuel had anointed him to be king. He was a refugee in the wilderness, hunted and in danger, yet he refused to take matters into his own hands. He exercised great self-control and forced his followers to do the same, until God "lifted me out of the slimy pit . . . [and] set my feet on a rock" (40:2). As a result David was joyful, and many others believed in the LORD (v. 3). "Blessed is the man who makes the LORD his trust, who does not look to . . . those who turn aside to false gods" (v. 4). Impatience with God or his church may cause a person to explore New Age or other cult-like expressions.

Isaiah tells us, "They who wait for the LORD shall renew their strength, they shall mount up with wings like eagles, they shall run and not be weary" (Isaiah 40:31 RSV). If we are patient, God will give us his strength. If we wait for him, we will feel uplifted in the Spirit. We will be able to move through life speedily without being tired.

109

We wear ourselves out trying to be God. If we allow God to be God, life is much easier. Waiting for God, resting in him, allows us to spend time with him, to hear his still, small voice. One word from God can cut through all our frantic anxieties.

1. Can you think of a time when you knew that God wanted you to wait for him and you did, and things worked out well?
2. Spend a few moments in his presence, asking him to relieve any burden you may have and to give you his peace.

The Blessings of a Positive Outlook

VERSES FOR THE WEEK
Let them give thanks to the Lord for his unfailing love
and his wonderful deeds for men, for he satisfies the
thirsty and fills the hungry with good things.
(Psalm 107:8-9)

Staying Away from the Ifs

DAILY READING Luke 15:11–32

A VERSE TO FOCUS OUR THOUGHTS
The younger one said to his father, "Father, give me my share of the estate."
So he divided his property between them. (v. 12)

If is a word that catapults us into fantasyland. It is the entrance point into unreality. It is Alice's "looking glass."

I remember being a member of a panel discussing the topic of fantasy for a television talk show. The moderator asked me if I had ever had a problem with fantasy. My answer surprised both him and me. I said, "Nothing serious, I just grew up in the nineteenth century." Since I had been unhappy during my teenage years, I reinvented the slower pace, the sense of community, the rural life of the farm on which my grandmother grew up. I disappeared through the doorway of "what if I had lived in the 1890s?" It was a momentarily pleasant but unrealistic and dead-end escape.

"If only" and "what if" are escape hatches from present reality. We convince ourselves that "if only" I had been born a girl; "if only" my parents were rich; "if only" I were beautiful, then I would be happy. "What if" I had a different boss? "What if" I could travel anywhere I wanted in the world? Then it would be a lot easier to be grateful. We tend to blame the people and the circumstances around us for our being dissatisfied with our lives.

The lost son had this problem. "What if" I were rich? "If only" I could get away from my father and his control, away from my brother and his sour face, I would be a free person. So he did get away, and he didn't become free. He got what he asked for, and he did what he wanted, but this didn't satisfy his inner longings for a happy life. God didn't figure into his plans—nor does he populate our fantasies, so they cannot possibly fulfill us either.

113

Are we unhappy with whom God made us? Are we discontent with our job—with what God has given us? The lost son discovered that the change required had to be *inside* him. It wasn't so much that his circumstances needed changing but that he himself did.

1. Are you content with the real world of your life? It is so easy to imagine a different scenario in which to live and lose touch with reality.

2. What are the "greener pastures" that are still able to attract you?

DAY TWO

Ingratitude is an Accusation Against God

DAILY READING Jonah 3-4

A VERSE TO FOCUS OUR THOUGHTS

[Jonah] prayed to the Lord, "O Lord, is this not what I said when I was still at home? That is why I was so quick to flee to Tarshish. I knew that you are a gracious and compassionate God, slow to anger and abounding in love, a God who relents from sending calamity."

(v. 4:2)

God created us to be grateful. By maintaining a right perspective on who God is and what he has done for us, we will be grateful. Gratitude is the testimony of a changed heart. We can be thankful for this particular thing and for that special person, but gratitude is a deeper appreciation, coming from a right relationship with God. It is the difference between having our lives built around a question mark or around an exclamation point.

Ingratitude, then, is an accusation against God. It is saying that he isn't who he says he is. It is like standing in a picket line, carrying a placard that reads, "God is treating me unfairly." "My life is a raw deal." "Beware of gods who advertise and don't deliver." What are our lives saying?

Jonah tried to run away from God, but he couldn't escape. God redirected him to Nineveh to pronounce judgment upon the enemy. He accepted his role as a prophet of doom. However, the people of Nineveh repented, and God honored their change of heart and spared them. Jonah was furious again and accused God of misusing him. There was no gratitude in Jonah because he was out of synch with God. He did not believe in forgiving his enemies and was not about to change. He might well have died a bitter man.

The one-talent servant in Jesus' parable could not live freely or gratefully either, because he too thought God was malicious and unfair. His life became an accusation, and this was expressed through his ingratitude. From time to time we should check to see what view of God our life is reflecting.

1. If you were really honest, would you say that God has given you a raw deal in some area of your life? Do you question his mercy? Do you wonder at his motives?

2. Is it possible that your life might be an accusation against God?

DAY THREE

Do You Desire to be Self-Sufficient?

DAILY READING Philippians 1:3–11

VERSES TO FOCUS OUR THOUGHTS
I thank my God every time I remember you.
In all my prayers for all of you, I always pray with joy.
(vv. 3-4a)

I grew up in a family that attempted to be self-sufficient. My grandparents' generation suffered serious reverses in the stock market crash of 1929. My parents struggled through the subsequent depression. I experienced the various deprivations of the Second World War. My family home was in the path of the racial riots of the 1960s. So we accumulated the firepower required to protect the property and bought enough land to grow our own food. The point was not to be dependent on "outside" help. Where was God in this picture? Self-sufficiency is an American myth. How we dream of being in control of our lives and not being indebted to anyone!

Gratitude springs from neediness—knowing that we can't defend ourselves, can't take care of ourselves, can't meet our own needs. It comes from an appreciation for other people's help. Paul told the Philippians that he thanked his God every time he remembered them. He was dependent on their help for the work of the gospel and therefore grateful to God for them. He longed for them from his prison in Rome.

Those of us who have learned from our need are often the most grateful. Have you noticed that mentally or physically challenged people often seem to be the happiest? They are more like the lilies of the field and the birds of the air because they know that God takes care of them.

Gratefulness comes from a realistic awareness of our need and of God's ability to meet that need, directly or through other people. Paul gives us his secret: "And my God will meet all your needs according to his glorious riches in Christ Jesus" (Philippians 4:19). These are the true grounds for gratitude.

1. Are you attempting to take care of your needs all by yourself? Are you proud of your self-sufficiency? Are you lonely?
2. Is there someone from whom you can seek help? Would you be willing to ask them for it?

DAY FOUR

God is the Source of All

DAILY READING 1 Corinthians 4:1–21

A VERSE TO FOCUS OUR THOUGHTS
For who makes you different from anyone else?
What do you have that you did not receive?
And if you did receive it, why do you boast as though you did not?
(v. 7)

Paul's argument to the Corinthians is convincing. "What do you have that you did not receive?" he asked them. It is obvious that we came into the world with nothing. What we have received since is all the gift of a loving heavenly Father. Even our strength and earning power are gifts of God. All that we have and are comes either directly from God, or is passed along to us as an inheritance from another person who received it as a gift from God. As David notes in Psalm 24:1, "The earth is the Lord's, and everything in it, the world and all who live in it." That includes each one of us.

If, then, we have received everything as a gift, Paul goes on to ask, "Why do you boast as though you did not?" Bragging about what we have or who we are is a contradiction. It betrays a misplaced sense of ownership. "Thank you" is the constant refrain of a grateful person who knows how much he owes. It would be good if we could go through the day continually saying, "Thank you, Jesus!" for all the little (and big) blessings of life. This would help to keep us in humble reality.

Not only is God the Creator and Sustainer of all things and all people, but also he is the Re-Creator, the Savior, of us all. Through his sacrificial life and death, he has secured for us our eternal well-being as Christians. Not until we get to heaven and see our King in his beauty (Isaiah 33:17), and look upon his "glorious scars," as Charles Wesley describes it, and realize that he will carry his human nature with him for eternity, will we fully appreciate what he has done for us. We will no longer need to be reminded to be grateful. We may be very sheepish that we were not more grateful in our life of anticipation here below.

1. Ask God to make you more aware of his many blessings during this day and then write these down this evening. Try this for the rest of this week.

2. Share with a friend what you have seen. What blesses an individual will bless others as well.

DAY FIVE

Gratitude is a Way of Life

DAILY READING Psalm 107:1–22

VERSES TO FOCUS OUR THOUGHTS
Let them give thanks to the Lord for his unfailing love
and his wonderful deeds for men,
for he satisfies the thirsty
and fills the hungry with good things.
(107:8-9)

Our negativity really is an attempt to protect ourselves from an "uncaring" God. We are afraid of being disappointed or rejected, so we refuse to get our hopes up. We hedge our bets in case God doesn't come through for us.

Numbers of times when I was a young boy, my dad was unable at the last minute to take me on a much-anticipated outing. I was devastated and, after a few such occasions, I refused to allow myself to get excited—about anything. I discovered that I had subconsciously placed my dad's picture on the face of God, not realizing that God cannot be equated with an earthly father. This boyhood decision, and numbers of self-protecting devices like it, had to be reversed in order for me to appreciate God for the faithful and caring Father that he truly is.

In Psalm 107 the psalmist spells out a succession of scenarios of how God delivered people when they cried out to him. Some were lost, some were imprisoned, some were afflicted, some were on the verge of shipwreck—but when they all cried out to the Lord in their trouble, he delivered them. There is a refrain at the conclusion of each section. "Let them give thanks to the LORD for his unfailing love" (8, 15, 21, 31). The point is thanksgiving. It is so easy to accept our blessings without acknowledging the One who gave them to us. We take for granted the blessings of daily life until our health or financial security is challenged. Gratitude is not meant to be reserved for dramatic events.

"Thank you" ought to be the framework through which we relate to God—genuine "thank yous," not just a preliminary nod that makes us feel less guilty about asking for more. Whenever we turn to God during the day, especially before meals, let us remember to thank him.

1. Think back over the past couple of days. Have you received each blessing with a refrain of thanksgiving? Placing your present circumstances in the context of thanksgiving can lift your spirits.
2. Do you pray before meals? Ask God to refresh your prayers.

DAY SIX
Gratitude is the Heart of Worship

DAILY READING   2 Chronicles 20:1–26

A VERSE TO FOCUS OUR THOUGHTS
After consulting the people,
Jehoshaphat appointed men to sing to the Lord and to praise him
for the splendor of his holiness as they went out at the head of the army,
saying: "Give thanks to the Lord, for his love endures forever."
(v. 21)

God's victories, big and small, were memorialized in worship. After the Israelites had passed through the Red Sea and stood on the far shore, watching the Egyptian army being drowned, Moses led them in worship (Exodus 15). Accompanied by tambourines and dancing, they sang what was to be known as the "Song of Miriam." Then they began their wilderness trek. After Deborah and Barak's great victory over Sisera and the Canaanite forces, the Israelites worshiped God in the Song of Deborah (Judges 5).

When a huge army from Edom came up to attack Judah in the days of King Jehoshaphat, the king publicly sought the Lord. God answered through a prophet and assured them that he would win this battle. They could go into battle without fear. So Jehoshaphat appointed singers to praise the Lord, and these worship leaders led the whole army forth to victory. "As they began to sing and praise, the LORD set ambushes. . . . " This is a great example of the power of worship. By faith we can thank God in advance for the fulfillment of his promises.

These scenes anticipate the ultimate heavenly victories over the forces of evil. The Lamb, looking as though it had been slain, stands in the center of the huge worshiping throng—the object of their praise and adoration. Scene after scene flashes before us as the worship continues, a litany of thanksgiving to our Lord and to his Christ. Eternal gratitude will never grow boring in the heavenly Jerusalem. May it not become boring here in our reflected worship.

Eucharist means thanksgiving. It suggests that receiving the Lord's Supper is the central expression of our corporate thanksgiving. In the liturgy, the prayer of preparation for communion is called the "prayer of thanksgiving." Here we remember to thank God for his inexpressible gift—Christ. When we focus on who God is, gratitude becomes natural.

1. Unless we approach worship with grateful hearts, endless versions of Sunday services don't make us eager for heaven. Perhaps asking God for a grateful heart would help make worship a more uplifting experience.
2. Is worship a regular part of your personal devotional time?

DAY SEVEN
How Can We Get There?

DAILY READING 1 Samuel 7:1–13a

A VERSE TO FOCUS OUR THOUGHTS
Then Samuel took a stone and set it up between Mizpah and Shen.
He named it Ebenezer, saying, "Thus far has the Lord helped us."
(v. 12)

Remembering is the key to gratitude. Recounting the history of God's faithfulness to us, not only as it is recorded in the Scriptures, but as we have personally experienced it, helps us to be thankful. Moses calls upon the Israelites in Deuteronomy to remember how God chose them when they were the fewest of peoples—delivering them and establishing them as a nation (Deuteronomy 7:7–9). I'll never forget my excitement when the reality of Jesus first burst in upon me!

After victorious wars we build monuments to our living heroes, and to our dead heroes as well. In the Old Testament men and women of faith built altars to express thanksgiving to God. Other stones, like those Joshua had erected at the Jordan River, and like the one that Samuel raised to commemorate the Israelite victory over the Philistines, stood as mute testimony to people's gratitude. Samuel named his stone "Ebenezer," or stone of help, to give a visible thank offering that "thus far has the LORD helped us" (1 Samuel 7:12). Perhaps we too can have visual memorials to remind us to be grateful.

I have a variety of stones serving as paperweights on my desk. These were culled from important moments in my life— a petrified rock from Arizona, a "dinosaur egg" from a Finger Lake glen, a stone washed smooth on a Martha's Vineyard beach. These constantly remind me of God's faithfulness.

Our Eucharist or communion service is our greatest remembrance service, a constant memorial raised to what Jesus has done for us.

Journaling is another way to memorialize God's goodness to us. We may keep an account of what we have asked of God, and add the date that it was answered, so that we have a ready-made litany of praise.

1. Perhaps you would like to dedicate a notebook to recording God's faithfulness in your life, keeping a list of what he has done for you.
2. Do you have things around your house that specifically remind you of God's miracles and blessings? Do other members of your family know what these mean to you?

Moving from a Sense of Failure into Grace

A VERSE FOR THE WEEK

Then I acknowledged my sin to you and did not cover up my iniquity. I said, "I will confess my transgressions to the Lord"—and you forgave the guilt of my sin.
(Psalm 32:5)

How Guilt Can be a Blessing in Disguise

DAILY READING Hebrews 10:19–25

A VERSE TO FOCUS OUR THOUGHTS
Let us draw near to God with a sincere heart in full assurance of faith,
having our hearts sprinkled to cleanse us from a guilty conscience
and having our bodies washed with pure water.
(v. 22)

I had to make an emergency trip to the dentist this morning because part of a back molar broke off during dinner last night, and as the evening went along my tooth began to ache. I suspect that I could have lived without that piece of tooth if I hadn't been afraid of the pain, so I prevailed upon my dentist to fit me in. He discovered that decay under the existing filling was destroying the enamel and that this had weakened the whole tooth. He also discovered that the tooth had a hidden fracture in it and was in danger of further disintegration. As a result I began to see that the pain that led to my panic had actually been my friend because it pointed to deeper, hidden problems that needed attention. After an hour in the dentist's chair I left his office quite relieved.

Thinking about this I realized that emotional and spiritual pain can also produce good results for us. They may make us feel bad for a time, and we naturally want to be rid of them, but they may be telling us that, like the tooth decay, there is something eating away in a hidden place inside us. Feelings of guilt are part of God's merciful warning system. They alert us like a light flashing on the dashboard of our souls, telling us that something will need attending to soon.

If we take our pain to Jesus he can help us see the underlying problem. He can clean out the offending decay and heal our inner fractures. He longs to forgive us, cleanse and reprogram our consciences, and to set us free again. Then the uncomfortableness of our pain will give way to the relief of being forgiven. Let us allow our failures, our disappointments, and our emotional pain to draw us closer to Jesus.

1. Are you feeling emotional pain? Are you struggling with a sense of failure? Are you discouraged about your present situation?
2. It is easy to allow these feelings to drag us down. We forget that Jesus stands ready to take them from us if we will give them to him. Do you have any feelings that you want to give to him right now? Will you let Jesus heal you?

DAY TWO
Condemnation is Not God's Way

DAILY READING Romans 8:1–17

A VERSE TO FOCUS OUR THOUGHTS
Therefore, there is now no condemnation for those who are in Christ Jesus.
(v. 1)

I find that I can go around under a nebulous cloud of condemnation much of the time if I allow myself to. I can easily feel secretly guilty and depressed. It's as if I have a little tape playing in my head, telling me over and over, "You are no good. You are a failure. Look at you! You can't even . . . There you go again, and again, and you call yourself a Christian?" At first I wonder if this is God speaking. Sometimes I need help to realize that I am only listening to my own commentary that arises from my own deep disappointment with myself. When I get down on myself like this there seems to be no end to oppressing thoughts.

I find that there is a crucial distinction between condemnation and conviction. Condemnation is actually a clever counterfeit of conviction. As with all counterfeits it looks and feels so much like the real thing, that we will be fooled if we are not careful. Condemnation rubs our noses in our problems and tells us that we are hopeless. We've been wrong again—we have failed and grace has run out this time.

Paul tells people like us, "Therefore, there is now no condemnation for those who are in Christ Jesus" (Romans 8:1). That statement comes trumpeting from the cross. No condemnation! None! Jesus has taken it away! We are not condemned! Condemnation is a trick of the enemy and we don't need to fall for it.

Conviction is the real thing. It comes from God. It has a clean feeling about it. It points out a specific problem and invites us to trust God in his mercy to specifically forgive us, and it is hopeful. Conviction is the way out of prison. Once we admit our failure, we can be forgiven. Condemnation leads to remorse, which is a dead-ended feeling sorry for ourselves. Conviction leads to repentance and a changed life. Praise God that he never condemns us! Our situation is never hopeless!

1. Are you feeling discouraged or hopeless? Perhaps you, too, are listening to the wrong voice. Jesus is never discouraged or hopeless about you, no matter how many times you fail.

2. Think for a few moments about how much Jesus has done for you—how many times he has forgiven you—how much he loves you.

DAY THREE
We Can't Make Our Failures Go Away

DAILY READING Psalm 32:1–11

A VERSE TO FOCUS OUR THOUGHTS
Then I acknowledged my sin to you and did not cover up my iniquity.
I said, "I will confess my transgressions to the Lord"
—and you forgave the guilt of my sin.
(v. 5)

It's almost an automatic reflex. My instinctive reaction is to try to fix myself, but the flip side of this is that I have again forgotten that I have a Savior who stands ready to relieve me of my burdens. I push down my feelings of failure and hide them under a flurry of frantic activity or behind non-stop surface conversation. But I find that my deeper feelings are like an inflated inner tube floating on water. No matter how hard I try, I just can't submerge it—it always pops up to the surface again.

Edgar Allen Poe wrote his short story "The Tell-Tale Heart" to illustrate these irrepressible feelings. The storyteller killed an old man, his hated companion, and buried him under the floorboards in his room. But the beating of his dead heart continued to resound so loudly in his ears, that when the police came he was forced to confess that he was guilty. The things that we have done will continue to harass us interiorly until we talk to Jesus about them.

I can attempt to rid myself of my feelings by excusing myself and accusing someone else. I can attempt to play with reality. I may actually sound convincing, and some people may believe me. I might have to avoid certain people, run away from certain situations, or perpetuate a succession of false appearances or even outright lie. It takes a lot of energy to live around my feelings of failure, and they don't go away.

David attempted to handle his adultery and murder in his own way, by burying them and frantically living above them. But God knew that this would eventually do him in. So in his mercy God sent the prophet Nathan to free him from the prison that he was building.

Once God had "lanced the boil," David was able to admit what he had done, to confess it before God, and to be forgiven and freed. We can hear his relief in Psalm 32:5: "Then I acknowledged my sin to you and did not cover up my iniquity. I said, 'I will confess my transgressions to the Lord'—and you forgave the guilt of my sin." What a relief! We need a Savior, and, praise God, we have the One who waits for us to turn to him!

1. Think of any place in your life where you are trying to live above your feelings of guilt.

2. Will you trust that God waits to forgive you and to set you free to find your success in him?

DAY FOUR

Confession:
God Invites Us to Come to Him

DAILY READING 1 John 1:5–10

A VERSE TO FOCUS OUR THOUGHTS
If we confess our sins,
he is faithful and just and will forgive us our sins
and purify us from all unrighteousness.
(v. 9)

Isaiah encourages us to accept this free invitation: "Let the wicked forsake his way and the evil man his thoughts. Let him turn to the Lord, and he will have mercy on him, and to our God, for he will freely pardon" (55:7). To "forsake" means to actively leave behind—to get rid of our useless baggage. We are to turn from our past failures and the thoughts that still bother us, with the assurance that God will forgive us, free us, and purify us.

I can be sure that he will forgive me. Moreover, I can know that he will change me so that I do not need to keep on failing. God has promised that to me, and I can take him at his word. No matter how many good resolutions I have made and broken, how many times I have made the wrong choice, God says he will still have mercy on me. Can I really believe that my continuing failure will be God's instrument for bringing me to confession, so that he can forgive and deliver me again? Why am I so slow to trust him?

Confession is the hinge on the doorway to forgiveness. It is the one sure relief. In confession we agree with God about who we are and what we have done, and we trust ourselves to his mercy. Only God through Jesus can take away our sin. Only he has made atonement for us. Why do we hesitate even for a moment? Why do we attempt to finesse our problems? Our failure should lead us to only one place—Jesus.

1. Are you feeling guilty about anything? Go quickly to Jesus and make your confession to him, before you talk yourself out of confessing your sin.
2. Let us believe that God "works all things together for our good," including our failures.

DAY FIVE

Do You Need Someone to Talk With?

DAILY READING James 5:13–20

A VERSE TO FOCUS OUR THOUGHTS
Therefore confess your sins to each other
and pray for each other so that you may be healed.
(v. 16a)

Why would I want to confess my faults to another person? Why not keep them to myself and confess them to God in private? Obviously, if I hurt another person, I may want to confess directly to that person and to seek her or his forgiveness. But why should I talk about the situation with someone who has nothing to do with it?

I personally find that sometimes God's forgiveness is hard to accept, especially for something that I consider serious or embarrassing. At other times it is hard to maintain an assurance of my forgiveness when I begin to doubt the genuineness of my contrition. Even if I can accept and maintain a sense of God's forgiveness, I may find it even more difficult to forgive myself. Another person may help give my forgiveness some greater and lasting reality.

At times I need someone who can help me see the seriousness of my sin, when I am tempted to minimize it. But more often I need someone who can help me accept the free mercy of God—to know that my faults are forgivable, and to believe that I am indeed forgiven.

I am writing somewhat apologetically here because many of you may, like me, have come from a tradition that discourages confession of this sort. Over the years I have come to learn the value of it. Presently I am going through a period of self-discovery that at times has been devastating. It is most encouraging to me to be able to talk regularly with an older man who has already discovered similar things about himself and can help me put into perspective what seems so difficult to accept about myself at the moment.

1. Do you have a behavior pattern in your life that you find difficult to accept and own up to, and for which it seems difficult to be forgiven?

2. Would you consider going to a wise counselor and having her or him help you see this from God's point of view?

DAY SIX

The Dangers of Harboring our Feelings

DAILY READING   Hebrews 12:14–29

A VERSE TO FOCUS OUR THOUGHTS
See to it that no one misses the grace of God
and that no bitter root grows up to cause trouble and defile many.
(v. 15)

When I was a boy scout our troop had a private camping area that we affectionately named "Camp Thorn," for obvious natural reasons. One day as I knelt down by the campfire, I felt a sharp pain in my right knee. I looked, and there, protruding from under the kneecap, was a stick. The scoutmaster removed it, I received first aid for the puncture wound, but over the next few weeks, the knee swelled and began to look ugly. I was feeling generally ill. My father took me to a doctor who immediately, in spite of my protests, made an appointment for me at the local hospital for the next morning.

That night my father attempted one final pre-hospital solution. He grabbed my knee in both of his hands and squeezed hard. I yelled, but to our astonishment a thorn, over an inch long, shot out from under the kneecap. The intense pain was brief. The hospital visit was no longer necessary.

My unacknowledged feelings can be like that hidden thorn, silently causing infection to spread throughout my body. Unconfessed sin patterns that remain within us can cause serious systemic problems. Our conscience can become insensitive, and we can do hurtful things without any feelings of regret. Chronic anxiety can also be caused by unresolved feelings.

How important it is for us to be willing to change! Repentance is a gift of God that frees us to change. When we turn around—change our mind—we return to the merciful hands of a loving God. He then can take from us that which offends him and others.

1. Do you have anything that is eating away inside of you, any grievance, any deep hurt, any secret habits?
2. It is easy for us to feel separated from God and to limit his mercy to our own understanding. Make a little leap of faith into his arms, and trust him to forgive and heal you.

DAY SEVEN
Such a Great Salvation!

DAILY READING Ephesians 2:1–10

A VERSE TO FOCUS OUR THOUGHTS
But because of his great love for us, God, who is rich in mercy,
made us alive with Christ even when we were dead in transgressions—
it is by grace you have been saved.
(v. 4)

Seeing how much our feelings affect us and sometimes hurt people around us, only points out what a great salvation Jesus has brought to us. That we can walk into a divine courtroom and plead guilty as charged—and have that confirmed by a heavenly jury—and then turn around and walk out free, is a miracle of grace. That the judge himself has served the sentence for us is beyond our ability to appreciate fully, at least in this life. Our problems may be great, but our God is greater.

There are no excuses needed, no oversights considered, no technicalities allowed to throw cases out of court. Full justice is rendered, and still we are free people. This is the mercy of our God. "I, even I, am he who blots out your transgressions, for my own sake, and remembers your sins no more" (Isaiah 43:25). He does it for his "own sake"—not because he is forced to, but because he wants to.

Paul eloquently expresses this to the Ephesians: "You were dead in your transgressions and sins, in which you used to live . . . gratifying the cravings of our sinful nature and following its desires and thoughts. Like the rest, we were by nature objects of wrath. *But because of his great love for us,* God, who is rich in mercy, made us alive with Christ even when we were dead in transgressions—it is by grace you have been saved (2:1–5, italics mine).

No matter how badly we have messed up, Jesus has paid the price. He has taken away our guilt. We don't have to continue to feel bad—we really don't. Even if we mess up over and over again, we still don't have to pay for it. Is this almost too good to be true? Yes. How hard it is for us to believe that we can receive such a great salvation absolutely free! It is there for the asking and the receiving.

1. How great is God's mercy to us! If you ask him, perhaps he would show you again—even give you a fresh picture of how great his mercy has been in your life.
2. Thank God that in Jesus he has paid the total price for your freedom! You can live like a liberated person.

Being Prepared to Declare What We Believe

A VERSE FOR THE WEEK
If you confess with your mouth, "Jesus is Lord,"
and believe in your heart that God raised him from the
dead, you will be saved.
(Romans 10:9)

Truth Comes from God

DAILY READING   Matthew 16:13–20

A VERSE TO FOCUS OUR THOUGHTS
Jesus replied, "Blessed are you, Simon son of Jonah,
for this was not revealed to you by man, but by my Father in heaven."
(v. 17)

Paul prayed for the Ephesians "that the eyes of your heart may be enlightened in order that you may *know* the hope to which he has called you" (1:18a, italics mine). He prays that light may dawn in their hearts so that they would *know* with an assurance that nothing could shake. How do you know that you are a Christian? You just know. Are you sure? Absolutely! Can anyone talk you out of it? Certainly not! This is the level of assurance that we can have about our faith.

How do we know that Jesus is alive and that he is God? The Spirit has revealed it to us. We know by the certainty of revelation. As Paul tells the Corinthians, we have received "the Spirit who is from God, that we may understand what God has freely given us" (1 Corinthians 2:12).

When Jesus asked his disciples if they knew who he was, Simon Peter replied, "You are the Christ, the Son of the living God" (Matthew 16:16). Or, as John records it, "We believe and *know* that you are the Holy One of God" (John 6:69, italics mine).

It is interesting that Jesus blessed Simon not so much because he now *knew*, but because of how he found out. Simon heard directly from the Father. The "eyes of his heart had been enlightened." He spoke with the authority of one who *knew* directly. This was a watershed moment in the Gospel accounts.

Truth worth basing our life upon comes through revelation. This kind of truth is not something that we have thought up or figured out. It is something God has revealed to us directly by his Spirit. Jesus longed for the day when his followers would have their own relationship with his Father, and he still does. When we hear from God and are willing to own up to our hearing from him, we please God.

l. Do you have any question about whether you are a Christian, or whether Jesus is God, or whether Jesus is alive? Ask God to reveal the truth to you so that you are settled about it.

2. Are you uncertain about any direction you are about to take? Ask God to give you his word about that as well.

DAY TWO

Declaring the Truth

DAILY READING Romans 10:5–15

A VERSE TO FOCUS OUR THOUGHTS
If you confess with your mouth, "Jesus is Lord,"
and believe in your heart that God raised him from the dead,
you will be saved.
(v. 9)

Jesus knew that it was very important for Simon Peter to hear directly from his Father, but it was also important for him to declare it verbally. Once Peter had made his confession publicly, Jesus then declared that he was going to establish his church so solidly that hell could not overcome it. Peter's confession was the basis upon which Jesus could build.

Faith is mysteriously secured and established by speaking. The Father spoke and creation came into being. Jesus spoke and his words created physical wholeness, or spiritual deliverance, or peace in storms. So Paul tells the Romans "that if you confess with your mouth, 'Jesus is Lord,' and believe in your heart that God raised him from the dead, you will be saved" (10:9). Belief and declaration go inseparably together. It is important that we testify to what we believe. This is how Jesus establishes his life in us.

Jesus also promised his followers, "Whoever acknowledges me before men, I will also acknowledge him before my Father in heaven" (Matthew 10:32). Our confessing Jesus publicly is recorded in heaven. Likewise Jesus goes on to say that if we disown him, he will disown us. Our spiritual well-being depends upon our testimony more than we might be aware.

Those who are called to lead other Christians have a special responsibility to be faithful to Jesus. We can share that which we know and have experienced, or that which we can anticipate experiencing shortly, because Jesus will hold us responsible to live what we say. Testimony and life go together.

> *1. No matter how strongly we profess our faith, if the rest of our words are not consistent, our testimony will have little impact. Is there talk coming out of your mouth that detracts from your testimony?*
> *2. How can you begin today to bring your words more into conformity with your Christian faith?*

DAY THREE
Our Life is Our Testimony

DAILY READING James 2:14–26

A VERSE TO FOCUS OUR THOUGHTS
In the same way, faith by itself, if it is not accompanied by action, is dead.
(v. 17)

Another obvious way to solidify our faith is by our actions. We can testify with our mouths, but how we act verifies the truth of what we say. It is most important that we live according to our own testimony. James is emphatic on this point: "Show me your faith without deeds, and I will show you my faith by what I do" (2:18b). Our faith is declared both by our mouths and through our lives. "Faith by itself, if it is not accompanied by action, is dead" (2:17).

I remember an illustration that I heard years ago. A man had stretched a high wire across the top of Niagara Falls. He took a wheelbarrow and asked a bystander if he believed that he could wheel it along the wire to the other side. The observer confidently said yes. The high-wire man replied, "Then, hop in." At this point the potential rider refused. If we declare that we believe Jesus is able, then we need to be prepared for the resulting invitation to trust him through our actions.

Action is true declaration. Abraham was called on to declare his faith in God by sacrificing his son, his only son, Isaac. All of God's promises depended on his one true son surviving, and yet God had asked Abraham to sacrifice him. Abraham truly believed God and was prepared to do as he asked. This willingness to obey established his faith, and James tells us that it made him righteous in God's sight.

Peter and John believed in Jesus and declared their faith publicly before the rulers, elders, and teachers in Jerusalem. But it was their actions that authenticated their message. When these leaders "saw the courage of Peter and John and realized that they were unschooled, ordinary men, they were astonished and they took note that these men had been with Jesus" (Acts 4:13).

What in our lives declares that we have been with Jesus? Our life is our ultimate statement of faith.

1. Our life speaks. Our testimony is who we are as much as what we say. Is there any way that what you do is not consistent with your faith?
2. If we are faithful, people will notice that we have been with Jesus. Thank God that he draws people to himself through you.

DAY FOUR

Let us Declare Together

DAILY READING 1 Timothy 3:14–16

A VERSE TO FOCUS OUR THOUGHTS
He appeared in a body, was vindicated by the Spirit,
was seen by angels, was preached among the nations,
was believed on in the world,
was taken up in glory.
(v. 16b)

It is important that we declare our faith publicly with other Christians. In many Christian traditions the congregation recites a creed, generally the Apostles' or Nicene Creed, during the Sunday morning worship service. This often follows the sermon and becomes, in essence, an affirmation of what was just proclaimed.

Early statements of faith or creeds are found in the New Testament, such as the one Paul writes to Timothy in our reading for today (1 Timothy 3:16). In the early church it became necessary to formulate beliefs into statements that would preserve the newly accepted tenets of faith. These were gathered together and became the embryonic form of our present-day creeds.

The Apostles' and Nicene Creeds were hammered out on the anvil of theological debate in those first centuries of the church. The Apostles' Creed (of uncertain dating) was crafted to repudiate the Gnostic view that Jesus was not fully man. The Nicene Creed (A.D. 325), the most universally used creed, was written as an apology against the Arian challenge that Jesus was not fully God. These creeds became the definition of orthodoxy and preserved the church against serious heresy. Thus on Sunday mornings we are making a centuries-old declaration of what we, in solidarity with orthodox Christian believers through the ages, believe.

Repeating and learning a creed is an anchor for us in this non-theologically oriented culture. It is a ready-made statement of what we believe, and by which we can evaluate the many groups that are propagating heterodoxy today. Paul tells Timothy to keep "the pattern of sound teaching, with faith and love in Christ Jesus. Guard the good deposit that was entrusted to you" (2 Timothy 1:13). I believe that reciting a creed is a way of doing this. I further believe that each time we stand together to declare our faith publicly we are making a small deposit in the bank of faith, and thus we are strengthening the universal church.

1. Can you recite from memory either the Apostles' or the Nicene Creed? If not, try to learn one of them.
2. Try writing a short statement of what you believe. Print it out and share it with a friend.

DAY FIVE

Gaining Victory Through Our Testimony

DAILY READING Revelation 12:7–12

A VERSE TO FOCUS OUR THOUGHTS
They overcame him by the blood of the Lamb
and by the word of their testimony;
they did not love their lives so much as to shrink from death.
(v. 11)

Paul reminds us that we are called to be "children of God without fault in a crooked and depraved generation, in which you shine like stars in the universe as you hold out the word of life" (Philippians 2:15b-16a). Here we are told that the world system around us is "crooked and depraved," no matter how good it may or may not look at the moment. We are like stars shining in this darkness, overcoming the world by the word of our testimony. Paul tells the Ephesians that the word of God spoken through them is like a sword (6:17b), and it is our only offensive weapon.

In Revelation the great cosmic battle is spread before us in dramatic detail, and we are shown God's ultimate victory. The dragon and his angels, who are capable of deceiving the whole world, are thrown down. A loud voice declared that the saints "overcame them by the blood of the Lamb and by the word of their testimony; they did not love their lives so much as to shrink from death" (Revelation 12:11). Our testimony to who God is, and to his faithfulness in our lives, is one of the three means of overcoming. We can wield our testimony against the enemy and defeat him by God's grace.

At times we may forget that we have entered into a great spiritual battle—that when we became Christians we automatically changed sides and joined the victorious army of God. We may forget that "our struggle is not against flesh and blood, but . . . against the powers of this dark world and against the spiritual forces of evil in the heavenly realms" (Ephesians 6:12). The victory has not yet been fully realized, so in the meantime we stand squarely on the truth of God that has been established in our lives—rooting out all darkness, all deception, all equivocating, and all confusion, and choosing, having "done everything, to stand" (Ephesians 6:13b).

People may out-argue us in the things of faith. They may be able to run circles around us intellectually, but they cannot take away our testimony, because it is the power of God in us. Every tongue that confesses that Jesus Christ is Lord brings the power of heaven to earth.

1. Ask God to remind you of the major victories in your life. Thank him that he has welcomed you to his side and has sustained you in the battle.

2. Ask him to help you stand on the truth. Rejoice that he has given you a testimony by which you can overcome the forces of this world.

DAY SIX

The Authority of Our Testimony

DAILY READING 1 John 1:1–7

A VERSE TO FOCUS OUR THOUGHTS

That which was from the beginning, which we have heard,
which we have seen with our eyes, which we have looked at
and our hands have touched—this we proclaim
concerning the Word of life.

(v. 1)

Our testimony is authenticated by what we have lived. When you are reading from a book or passing along second-hand information, as profound as it may be, there may be little personal validation. When you know from the depths of your being that what you are saying is true for you, there is an accompanying power to convict, because you and the Holy Spirit are witnessing together.

George Beverly Shea, the revered soloist on the Billy Graham Crusade Team, was asked about how much he knew of God. His reply caught my attention. "Not much," he said, "but what I do know has changed my life." As long as everything we know has an accompanying change in our lives we will have spiritual authority.

This is the genius of Alcoholics Anonymous, or of other similarly patterned support groups. People share their testimonies of how their lives have been changed, and other lives are changed just through the hearing.

Recently a group was attempting to help a woman who was in the midst of an angry tirade. Not long before, she had

144

attended an anger-management clinic, but had lost control again. Some in the group tried to shout her down, some tried to defeat her arguments, some tried to deny her accusations. Then another woman stepped forward and spoke calmly but firmly, telling this woman what she was feeling and why she felt that way, and showing her how not to trust her feelings at the moment. To our amazement the angry woman agreed and calmed down. The speaker had also struggled with a serious anger problem and had attended a similar clinic. She didn't have to say so; she just knew the situation from her own experience and could speak with the authority of her life.

That is why Jesus came—so he would know, and his testimony would have the authority of the experiences of a human life. That is why John's testimony was so powerful: "That which we have heard, which we have seen with our eyes, which we have looked at and our hands have touched—this we proclaim concerning the Word of life" (1 John 1:1). Let us speak with confidence about what we know.

1. If we have been through a situation, then we can more easily help those who are going through a similar one. It's not our eloquence or our superior knowledge that helps the other person, it is our validation of the other's experience. You may be able to help someone if you share your story.
2. Would you be willing to give your testimony to someone this week?

DAY SEVEN
Witnessing to the Truth of Christ

DAILY READING 1 Peter 3:13–22

A VERSE TO FOCUS OUR THOUGHTS
But in your hearts set apart Christ as Lord.
Always be prepared to give an answer to everyone who asks you
to give the reason for the hope that you have.
(v. 15)

So do not be ashamed to testify about our Lord" (2 Timothy 1:8a). Are we fearful of speaking about Jesus? Are we hesitant to tell someone what Jesus has done for us? Lots of Christians are.

Peter and John, in the midst of being reprimanded by the authorities in Jerusalem, testified, "We cannot help speaking about what we have seen and heard" (Acts 4:20). Peter would say later on, "Always be prepared to give an answer to everyone who asks you to give the reason for the hope that you have" (1 Peter 3:15). In my college fellowship there was an eager new Christian who always greeted us in the morning by asking us if we had a fresh word from the Lord for the day. We made sure we had something before we left our dormitory rooms. Can we trust God to give us an answer to every question about our faith? It might be helpful to have something specifically in mind.

My wife and I have a testimony of how God sustained us over many years with almost no resources, and yet we never ran out of money. Recently we were in a meeting where we had opportunity to talk about financial experiences and fears. At the end of the time we suddenly realized that we had not given our testimony of God's faithfulness to us. I felt almost like I was betraying him, so I blurted out our story. Why am I so slow to speak about what God has done for me?

If you, too, are shy about speaking, I would suggest that you do something that helped me. Write out a simple version of your story, short enough to fit on one page. Print it out in an appealing format, and make it available to people with whom you come in contact. It will have appeal to people just because you wrote it.

1. Write out a simple version of your testimony and give it to someone.

2. Get together with this person and share your stories.

Healing Wounded Relationships

A VERSE FOR THE WEEK

All this is from God, who reconciled us to himself
through Christ and gave us the ministry of reconciliation.
(2 Corinthians 5:18)

How Conviction Leads to Reconciliation

DAILY READING Luke 15:11–32

A VERSE TO FOCUS OUR THOUGHTS
The son said to him, "Father, I have sinned against heaven and against you.
I am no longer worthy to be called your son."
(v. 21)

The story of the Prodigal Son pivots on the phrase "when he came to his senses." The younger son had taken his father's inheritance, separated from his father, and then proceeded to prove that he could not handle life on his own. We find him in poverty and desperate need, living among the pigs. There it was that his eyes were opened. Suddenly he could see what his father could see, and he was enabled to take responsibility for what he had done. He had been wrong; his plan failed.

There are moments of conviction in our lives when we suddenly realize that our motives are wrong. I had such a moment yesterday. I suddenly recognized that my drive to prove myself at a new job was nothing nobler than an attempt to prove my father wrong. I acknowledged that I didn't have to show him I could do it, and the stress level went down dramatically. I was free to relax and be a real person rather than an uptight competitor who in the process was thwarting his higher goals.

Conviction flashes up in a moment and leads to definite action. Rather than consign the son to a lifetime of feeling bad in a distant country, it sent him home in realistic need and hopefulness. Close relationships are important, but they can be sources of either great blessing or great hurt. God has made us vulnerable to one another. Accumulated hurts will destroy relationships, so we must protect them for the treasures they are.

The father's actions in the story speak of total forgiveness. Acknowledging that the son was wrong, he neither excused him nor accused him. At the moment of the son's confession the enmity was over. The relationship was reconciled—restored to a new level of intimacy and celebration.

1. Are you at odds with anyone? Then it is important to work toward reconciliation. Ask God to help you see this relationship from his point of view.
2. Are you harboring unforgiveness, rehearsing hurts, or seeking subtle revenge? Again, ask God to help you turn around.

DAY TWO
"Be Reconciled to God"

DAILY READING 2 Corinthians 5:16–6:2

A VERSE TO FOCUS OUR THOUGHTS
We implore you on Christ's behalf: Be reconciled to God.
(v. 20b)

God made reconciliation available to us in Christ. Christ pleads with us to come to the cross and be received back into the arms of a waiting Father, just as the Prodigal Son was. "For God was pleased . . . through him to reconcile to himself all things . . . by making peace through his blood, shed on the cross." (Colossians 1:19-20)

Through a moment of convicting insight we are enabled to turn from our own self-centered ways and accept Jesus as our Savior and Lord, and bow in humble worship before him. God's anger has been turned away; justice has been rendered; mercy is available, and our sin is forgiven. The dividing curtain has been torn in two from the top to the bottom, and we are free to boldly enter God's presence. We belong to a forgiving God. This is our great salvation.

But this same pattern is established as an ongoing process for the Christian life. Often God overrules our cherished plans and asks us to do things we would not choose to do. When we find it necessary to give up things we feel are essential to our well-being, we are apt to get mad at him. Sometimes it is hard for us to admit that we are angry with God. The thought of forgiving God is foreign to our theology, but from our aggrieved position it might be a starting point for breaking down our re-erected dividing curtain. Once we do this we may discover that what God has done has reminded us of what a parent or parent-like figure used to do, and that he or she is the one we really need to forgive.

1. Can you admit to being angry with God? Is there an area of your life where you are mad at him at the moment?
2. Ask God to show you his mercy and his love again so that you can become reconciled with him once more.

DAY THREE

Reconciling with the Past

DAILY READING Ephesians 2:14–22

VERSES TO FOCUS OUR THOUGHTS
For he himself is our peace,
who has made the two one and has destroyed the barrier,
the dividing wall of hostility.
(v. 14)

Throughout history there have been many long-standing national and ethnic animosities. Some of us have been born into these and have been encouraged to perpetuate them. Paul wrote about this kind of division between the Jews and the Gentiles: "For he himself is our peace, who has made the two one and destroyed the barrier, the dividing wall of hostility"

(Ephesians 2:14). God has already provided for the reconciliation of all divisions among peoples through his Son, after this prototype of the Jew-Gentile feud. He is always at work to realize this healing among nations and peoples with histories of division. Reconciliation in this sense is not bound by time or space.

This is as true for individuals as it is for groups. Jesus can heal us from long-standing memories of past events and personal hurts. He can take us back in time and overlay his healing love on the unreconciled events and relationships that continue to affect us, if we are willing. This can even be true for those with whom we can no longer communicate—those who suffer from dementia and can no longer cope mentally, or those who have died. They are with Jesus and so are we. He is the reconciling relationship that spans the gulf of death. He can let these persons know that we have forgiven them. This is specifically true with cases of physical, emotional, and sexual abuse. It may take many sessions of therapy, and a number of partial attempts, before we are truly ready to forgive and release a person who has greatly harmed us. But God can make good to us even the most painful experiences of our past if we offer them to him.

Remember that we can be bound to and by people we have not forgiven. We have given them access to our interior life where, by withholding forgiveness, we allow them to steal our peace. Forgiving them releases us and unlocks our prison doors, so that we can more fully respond to Jesus.

1. Are you still affected by past hurts and circumstances? Is there anyone whom you need to forgive in order to get free of this past?

2. Ask God to give you the grace to give up any desire to get even.

DAY FOUR
Reconciling in the Present

DAILY READING   Matthew 5:21–26

A VERSE TO FOCUS OUR THOUGHTS
Leave your gift there in front of the altar.
First go and be reconciled to your brother;
then come and offer your gift.
(v. 24)

Although we may have long-standing relationships and situations that require reconciliation, this should not camouflage the need to stay current in our present-day relationships. Life within a lively fellowship constantly pulses between hurt or anger and reconciliation, because we become vulnerable to one another. Jesus urges us to keep short accounts.

As we approach God in worship our relationships should be reconciled. Jesus tells us that if we arrive at a worship service and suddenly remember that we are at odds with another member of the fellowship, we are not to resort to a memory device such as changing a ring from one hand to the other. We are to go then! Make this a priority. Interrupt what you are doing and take care of the broken relationship. It is important to Jesus that we do so.

Some groups take Jesus so seriously that they actually schedule a time for this in their worship services. A vestige is experienced in other traditions through the "passing of the peace." Offering the peace of the Lord to a person is an action of reconciliation. Perhaps, then, if our church fellowship follows this practice we ought to search out persons with whom we have had some difficulties—making the passing of the peace an intentional act of reconciliation.

Spontaneous, unself-conscious, and unself-protective relationships give freedom to the Spirit. Unreconciled relationships lead to hiding behind an image, monitoring our conversations, and

155

carefully crafting responses so as not to leak our true feelings. The Spirit is stifled, and everyone feels superficial and uptight.

A vulnerable fellowship is a jewel of the kingdom. Our fellowship should be like a "Sinners Anonymous"—a safer place than a bar room or an addiction support group to work out present relationships. So let us "settle matters quickly" (Matthew 5:25).

1. How about picking up the telephone right now and getting something straightened out with someone in your fellowship?
2. Is there someone in your fellowship with whom you relate only superficially? Can you do something about this?

DAY FIVE

"Seventy Times Seven"

DAILY READING   Colossians 3:5–17

A VERSE TO FOCUS OUR THOUGHTS
Bear with each other and forgive whatever grievances you may have against one another. Forgive as the Lord forgave you.
(v. 13)

Now let's think more specifically about the need to forgive someone who comes to us asking for forgiveness. To forgive someone from our heart may be as difficult, and as embarrassing, as to admit that we are the wrong one and ask for another person's forgiveness.

In the first place, we need to admit that we have been hurt and that the other person is wrong. We can't excuse them or let them off the hook by saying something like, "We are all like that." When someone asks us, "Will you please forgive me?" they are asking a vulnerable question, and the only proper and satisfying answer is a thoughtful and sincere, "I forgive you."

Second, to truly and permanently forgive someone may take some serious work on our part. Paul says, "Forgive whatever grievances you may have against one another. Forgive as the Lord forgave you" (Colossians 3:13). That last command is the stickler. To revisit the comment made by Corrie ten Boom—she read, "You . . . hurl all our iniquities into the depths of the sea" (Micah 7:19b), and then she said, "He puts up a little sign saying, 'No fishing!'" When we truly forgive, we forfeit the right to bring up that sin ever again. Every time our feelings of hurt and anger come up, we need to forgive the person again until those feelings no longer rise up.

Third, even if the person sins continually against us, if they sincerely ask for forgiveness each time, Jesus commands us to forgive. Peter thought seven times would be a good limit, but Jesus raised him seventy-fold (Matthew 18:21-22). In other words, there is no limit. We need to live in an atmosphere of forgiveness. Forgiveness then becomes not so much an act, as a way of life.

Putting an exclamation point behind this, Jesus says that if we refuse to forgive and hold anything against a brother, we jeopardize our heavenly Father's forgiving us (Mark 11:25). How important it is for us to forgive!

1. Is there someone who consistently hurts you? Have you "run out" of forgiveness? Ask God for help.
2. Don't be surprised if you have to continually forgive someone who has hurt you deeply, even if they don't ask for our forgiveness.

DAY SIX
Being Reconciled with Family Members

DAILY READING Genesis 33:1–20

A VERSE TO FOCUS OUR THOUGHTS
But Esau ran to meet Jacob and embraced him;
he threw his arms around his neck and kissed him. And they wept.
(v. 4)

Family members have the greatest influence on most of us. They have the most potential for either blessing or hurt, or for both at the same time. Members of our immediate families are often the most difficult to forgive and to mean it. As we grow older we continually find new levels on which we have been affected. Forgiveness and reconciliation among family members are the most important and precious gifts we can offer or receive.

Jacob cheated his twin brother, Esau, on two major occasions. In his fear of retribution he ran away from home and stayed away for twenty years. Now with great trepidation and humiliation he was returning home. "But Esau ran to meet Jacob and embraced him; he threw his arms around his neck and kissed him" (Genesis 33:4). Stop the motion picture right there. I am surprised (as I think about it) that I don't ever remember having seen a painting of that emotional scene of reconciliation that changed both of their lives forever.

We have a similar picture of Joseph's throwing his arms around Benjamin, kissing all his brothers and weeping over them (Genesis 45)—a great emotional reconciliation after many years of estrangement. The snapshot of the Prodigal returning and being hugged by his father captures the same freedom through reconciliation between family members.

Oh, that this were more common! We rise emotionally above this kind of thing, denying the hurts and refusing to accept reality. This is too painful, we say. Years ago I went to my mother after I was convicted that though I had relied on a "good boy" camouflage, I was really a hurtful son, and in my self-centeredness I had treated her shabbily. She could neither understand what I was saying nor see anything for which to forgive me. I found that very difficult. She was well meaning, but she didn't understand the Christian life the way I did. It is important as Christians to accept any family member who attempts to reconcile with us, even if we don't see things the same way.

1. Are you estranged from any member of your family?
2. Is there anything you can do to help bring about reconciliation?

DAY SEVEN
Going the Extra Mile

DAILY READING Matthew 5:38–48

A VERSE TO FOCUS OUR THOUGHTS
But I tell you, Do not resist an evil person.
If someone strikes you on the right cheek, turn to him the other also.
(v. 39)

Jesus suggests that reconciliation should be a lavish experience. It is not to be done begrudgingly or skimpily. It is not a standard-sized commodity and doesn't fit in neat packages. It is more like the spring of living water welling up to eternal life—like the ointment with which the woman anointed the feet of Jesus—unmeasured, uncalculated, overflowing, and socially outlandish. It is Esau, not politely and dignifiedly shaking hands with his usurping brother, but throwing his arms around his neck and kissing him. It is a hands-on, spontaneous, exuberant expression of love.

This is the overflowing mercy of Jesus——the tree filled with white ribbons announcing that the hesitantly returning outcast is overwhelmingly welcomed home. This is passing on the grace of reconciliation that we have received through Jesus.

Aggressive reconciliation is not limited to an even exchange. It doesn't resist an evil person. It turns the left cheek when it is struck on the right cheek (Matthew 5:39). It gives without expectation of a return.

Paul tells us that God has given us the ministry of reconciliation (2 Corinthians 5:18). This means going the extra mile by not allowing a person to be at odds with us, no matter how provocative that person may be. If we are constantly prepared to forgive we will present the need for future reconciliation. It takes two to fight, and we can remove ourselves from the fray. God give us the grace to aggressively minister reconciliation.

1. Is there anyone in your life who is demanding more of you than you want to give?
2. Ask God to help you care for this person before you begin to resent her or him.